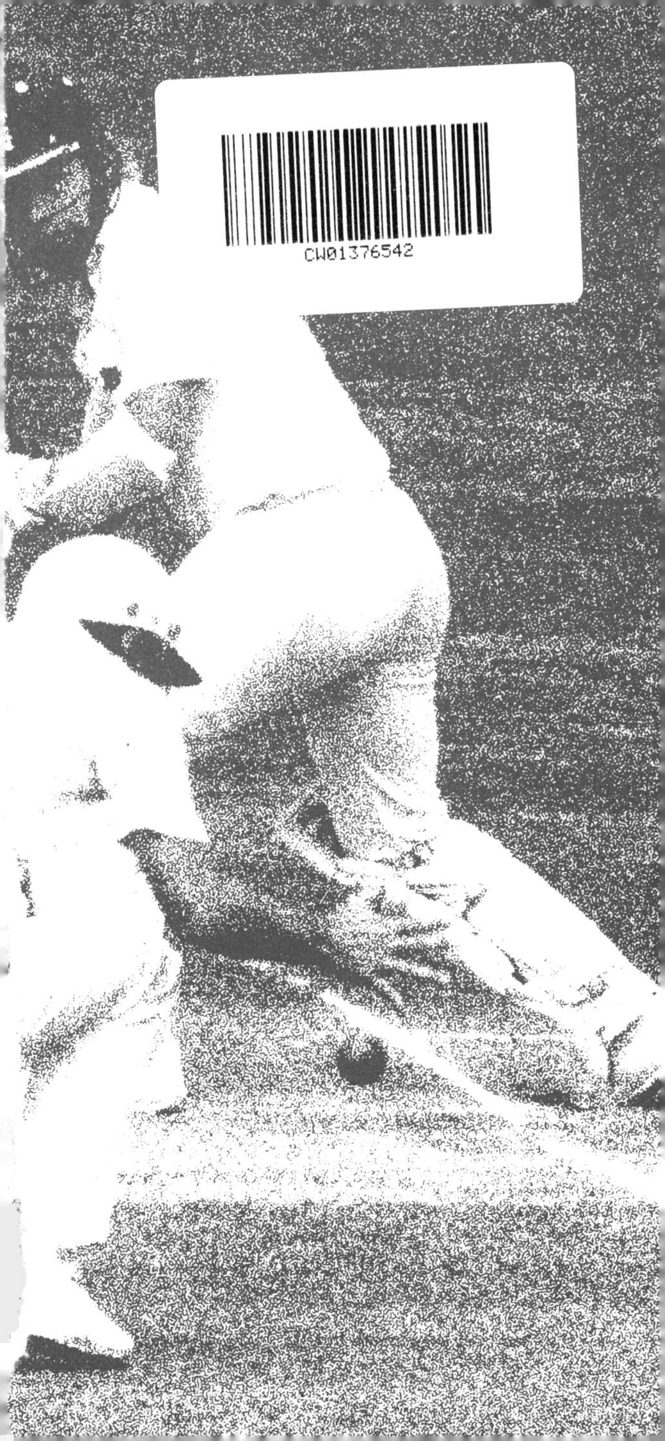

Daily Telegraph

POCKET SPORTS FACTS

CRICKET

MICHAEL MELFORD
BILL FRINDALL

Consultant Editor: Norman Barrett

Editor: Gill Freeman

Design: Nigel Standerline

Designed and produced by
Autumn Publishing Ltd.,
10 Eastgate Square, Chichester,
West Sussex.

Published by Telegraph Publications,
135, Fleet Street,
London EC4P 4BL

Statistics © Bill Frindall
© 1984 Daily Telegraph
and Autumn Publishing Ltd.

Typesetting by Project Reprographics, Chichester.
Printed by CGP Delo, Yugoslavia.

ISBN 0 86367 017 2

All rights reserved. No part of this publication may be reproduced, stored in a retrieval system or transmitted, in any form or by any means, electronic, mechanical, photocopying, recording or otherwise, without the prior permission of the copyright owner.

Cover Picture: Ian Botham
*Picture credits:
All-Sport, BBC Hulton Picture Library, Colorsport, Bill Smith*

CONTENTS

- **4 INTRODUCTION**
- **6 TEST CRICKET**
- **12 TEST CRICKET RECORDS**
- 12 Summary of All Test Matches 1876-77 to 1983
- 14 Team Records
- 16 Batting Records
- 19 Bowling Records
- 23 Wicket-Keeping Records
- 24 Fielding Records
- 25 All-Round Records
- 26 Other Records
- 27 Career Records of Current Test Players
- **30 GREAT CRICKETERS**
- **64 THE WORLD CUP**
- **68 FIRST-CLASS CRICKET RECORDS**
- 68 Team Records
- 76 Individual Records
- 76 Batting
- 86 Bowling
- 90 All-Round Performances
- 93 Wicket-Keeping
- 94 Fielding
- 96 Career Records
- 100 First-Class Competitions
- **104 TEST GROUNDS**
- 104 Australia
- 106 England
- 109 South Africa
- 110 West Indies
- 111 New Zealand
- 113 India
- 114 Pakistan
- 115 Sri Lanka
- **116 CAPTAINCY AND ITS SIGNIFICANCE**
- **118 THE LAWS OF CRICKET**
- **126 CRICKET TERMS**

INTRODUCTION

One of the quirks and, on the whole, attractions of cricket is that it is followed with such varying knowledge by so many people. Not until you are interrogated about the phenomenon of cricket by a 'foreigner' who does not know a stump from a bail, do you realise that total ignorance of the game is hard to achieve in Britain and the Commonwealth, so deep are its roots there.

The natives of these areas, however hard they may protest, some of them, that they are uninterested in cricket and know nothing about it, have been unable to avoid assimilating some vague idea of its spirit and purpose. From this level of interest upwards, ever upwards, there are degrees of cricket knowledge, steps up an unending staircase, for no one can ever know everything about cricket.

It may not always be realised that cricket, like bowls and snooker, is very much a game of the old Empire. Other games and pastimes originating in Britain have spread throughout the world. They play rugby at the highest level in France and Rumania. They play hockey all over the Continent. They row with zest and expertise in eastern Europe. But with the honourable exceptions of Holland and Denmark, no country unpopulated at some stage in its history by the evangelistic British sportsman, has played organised cricket with any regularity.

Suppose the Empire builders of the 18th and 19th centuries had reached out even further. What other Worrells, Weekeses, Walcotts, what other Sobers, might have graced the world's cricket fields if the British had colonised not only Barbados but neighbouring Martinique?

It remains a curiosity that soccer, which more than any other

Australia's 'run machine' Sir Donald Bradman, the most prolific batsman in the history of the game.

game has spread throughout the world from its origins in England, is not played at a comparable level in the very countries which took to cricket so readily—Australia, New Zealand, South Africa, India, Pakistan and the West Indies. Why not?

Partly, perhaps, it is because cricket is an older game than soccer and took root first in the developing countries of the 19th century. WG Grace was making hundreds of runs for Gloucestershire and visiting Australia before Tottenham Hotspur played a match.

Yet among the millions who follow cricket with varying degrees of intensity in England and other Commonwealth and former Commonwealth countries, few know much about the game's history—its origins on the borders of Kent and Sussex; the extraordinary years in the mid-18th century when the famous players of the day were those of a Hampshire village team, the men of Hambledon; the founding of MCC and its growing influence; the All England XI; the feats of WG, of Fry and Ranji and Hobbs and later of Bradman; the birth and slow development of international cricket; its recent expansion. To many, perhaps, cricket did not exist before television.

In the same way, many who lean against the bar and passionately advocate or decry the claims of X or Y to play for England may never have seen a first-class match. Others who offer opinions on the state of the game may be hugely knowledgeable, if not of its history, then of its statistics or technique or its personalities—perhaps even of all four.

Between these two extremes is a vast diversity of knowledge of cricket and of interest in the game. This book may perhaps inform some in that great divide.

Sir Garfield Sobers, West Indies captain and arguably the finest all-rounder the game has known.

TEST CRICKET

Test match cricket was not known as such at its inception which was with an International match played between England and Australia in Melbourne in March 1877. The name was acquired as an interchange of visits developed between the two countries. The Ashes soon became the mythical prize for series between England and Australia, as a result of a notice in the *Sporting Times* of 30th August, 1882, following the first defeat by Australia of a full strength England team in England. The 'obituary' notice destined to become famous read:

> In affectionate remembrance of English cricket which died at The Oval, 29th August 1882, deeply lamented by a large circle of sorrowing friends and acquaintances. R.I.P.
> N.B. The body will be cremated and the Ashes taken to Australia.

In the following year, after England had defeated Australia in Sydney, some ladies burnt a stump and sealed the ashes in an urn, presenting it to the England captain, the Hon Ivo Bligh, later Lord Darnley. In his will Lord Darnley bequeathed the urn to the Marylebone Cricket Club and since 1927 it has remained at Lord's, irrespective of who wins the series.

THE DEVELOPMENT OF TEST CRICKET

Test cricket was extended in 1888-89 when England, captained by CA Smith, better known in later years as the Hollywood film actor C Aubrey Smith, played South Africa in Port Elizabeth, but it was another 40 years before other countries were strong enough to challenge these three. In the meantime England and Australia exchanged visits, no less than seven in the 1890s, a remarkable number considering the slowness of travel in those days.

England went four more times to South Africa before South Africa felt strong enough to send a side to England. This they did in 1907, returning in 1912 to take part in a triangular tournament with England and Australia. The tournament was not a success. The weather was unhelpful, Australia, because of domestic differences, sent a half-strength side and South Africa who had done well with a strong hand of spin bowlers on their previous visit, proved weaker this time. The experiment has never been repeated.

After the First World War both Australia and South Africa continued to alternate series home and away with England and met each other for the first time towards the end of 1921 when WW Armstrong's Australian team stopped in South Africa on the way home from a triumphant tour of England.

England's early tours of Australia—not always with a full strength side, for amateurs could not always take six months or more away from their work—were organised by private individuals and it was not until 1903-04 that MCC took over the management of official touring teams. In the winter of

1929-30, for the only time, they sent two sides overseas to play Test matches, in West Indies and New Zealand. West Indies had already played their first Test matches in England 18 months earlier. New Zealand played, and lost, their first Test with England in Christchurch in January 1930.

Thereafter both West Indies and New Zealand came twice to England before the Second World War. England fell into the pattern of visiting New Zealand after a long tour of Australia, which had economical advantages but was never wholly successful because of the atmosphere of anti-climax attending it on the England side.

In 1932 India played their first Test match and though England won this match at Lord's and a series in India in 1933-34, the latter win was their last in India for 43 years. On the partition of India after the Second World War, Pakistan became the seventh Test-playing country, beginning with a visit to India in 1952-53 and another to England in 1954. The only other country to attain Test match status subsequently was Sri Lanka who began with a Test match against England in Colombo in 1982.

By this time, however, there were still only seven Test-playing countries as South Africa dropped out after leaving the Commonwealth in 1960. One of the requirements of the Imperial Cricket Conference, the only international association of cricket and a forum for exchange of views rather than a governing body, had been that the member-countries should be members of the Commonwealth. Though South Africa had been founder-members with England and Australia, no provision existed for them to continue in the Conference. By the time Pakistan left the Commonwealth the constitution of the ICC had been changed, indeed its title had become the International Cricket Conference, and they were not required to leave.

The playing of Test series has not necessarily been tied to membership of the ICC but has been a matter for arrangement between the two countries involved. Thus during the 1960s, after leaving the ICC, South Africa visited both Australia and England and received teams from New Zealand and England once and Australia twice. But as a result of international pressure their four-match Test series against Australia in 1970, which they won 4-0 by huge margins, was the last they played. They stepped down from Test cricket at a time when they had never been stronger, indeed were probably the best in the world.

The conditions of play in Test matches have always been a matter for the two sides, but with more frequent series between the Test-playing nations made possible by air travel and made desirable for financial reasons, there has tended to be greater uniformity.

The first Test matches in Australia were played over four days but in England, where a longer day's play was customary, three days were considered enough. The only Test of 1887-88 in Melbourne ran to five days, the normal duration nearly 100 years later. However, Test matches in Australia grew longer in the 20th century. Many in the early 1900s occupied six days. England stuck to three days even after the First World War, moving up to four only for the Ashes series of 1930. This at once produced a famous Test match at Lord's in which Austrlaia replied to England's 425 with 729 for six declared and then bowled England out again for 375, leaving themselves plenty of time to win by seven wickets on the fourth afternoon.

By this time Australia were favouring timeless Tests. Three of the five in 1924-25 went to seven days and the last of 1928-29 to eight days. A year later this record was beaten in Kingston, Jamaica, when the last match of a four-Test series was due to be played to a finish as each side had won once. In fact, rain prevented play on the eighth and ninth days and the match was abandoned as a draw because the England team had to sail home.

It was a similar match in Durban, the last Test match played outside England before the Second World War, which put an end to the 'timeless' match. The series between South Africa and England had been of four-day matches of which England had won one. The playing conditions ruled that as there was a difference of only one match so far, the Fifth and last Test should be played to a finish.

South Africa made 530 to which England replied with 316. South Africa increased their lead by 481 before they were bowled out in the second innings. This left England needing 696 to win, still nearly 300 more than any side has made in the last innings to win a Test match. But the reasonable expectations that the pitch would have deteriorated by the time England set about their task were not fulfilled. It had rained at intervals during the match, not only at night but during the eighth day when no play was possible. This had meant that day after day the pitch rolled out better than ever and on the tenth day, England at 496 for three needed only another 200 with seven wickets standing. But it rained again and as England had to leave to catch their boat home, the match was left drawn after ten days with the score 654 for five. This was enough to banish the idea of timeless Test matches for good.

England resumed after the War with three-day matches in England against India and New Zealand, four days against South Africa and five against Australia, but after New Zealand, with a strong batting side, had held them to a series of four drawn matches in 1949, the duration of Tests in England was standardised at five days. Countries in warmer climates where it had been customary to play for only five, or five and a half, hours each day increased this eventually to six hours, and a five-day Test match of six hours became almost uniform throughout the world, with an extra day sometimes added if the series was level or if the difference was only one match.

Just as the length of the matches has varied, so has the number of balls in the over, which has usually been the same as has applied in first-class cricket in the host country. Thus for many years until the late 1970s Test matches were played in Australia with eight-ball overs. England's only flirtation with the eight-ball over was with a two-year experiment begun in 1939. It was cut off by the outbreak of war after one season and this was considered enough to have established that it was not an improvement on the six-ball over. It has not been tried again in England.

Whether or not the pitch should be left uncovered during a match is another subject on which different views have been held. England, despite its capricious climate, has been the most keen to leave pitches open, either throughout the match or during the hours of play, in the belief that covering detracts from the character of the game. However, by the 1980s full covering was the norm in Test cricket.

THE STRATEGY OF TEST MATCHES

The advent of limited-over cricket which began in the 1960s and developed in the 1970s—especially in Australia where television and the ability to play under floodlights on balmy summer evenings were powerful influences—has not greatly affected the popularity of Test cricket which continues to be the ultimate trial of strength between two countries. The playing of a match over five days allows the game to unfold, often fluctuating unpredictably, as the captains of bowling sides devise ways to dismiss the opposing batsmen—perhaps by changes of bowling or adjustments of field-placing.

Here lies the great weakness of the limited-over game. In that, the fielding side does not have to bowl the other side out, merely to restrict it to as few runs as possible in the allotted number of overs. Hence the defensiveness of the bowling and field-placing in limited-over cricket.

In conventional cricket, most of all in a match with the duration of a Test match, the main object of a fielding side is to bowl their opponents out. The captains are not tied, as the captain in a limited-over match is, by restrictions on the number of overs which the bowler can bowl or in the placing of his fielders. The Test captain cannot rely on the opposing batsmen taking risks as his side's innings reaches a certain point. He must scheme the batsman's undoing. In the same way, the batsman is not bound to attack at a certain time. He may do so at any time if he thinks that domination of the bowling can be achieved with reasonable safety.

Through this freedom of choice of captains, batsmen and bowlers is derived the charm, character and variety which is at the heart of cricket. It is a basic reason why it remains a game played and watched with unflagging enthusiasm and keen

TEST CRICKET

partisanship in those many parts of the world where British settlers, soldiers or traders introduced it.

It is Test cricket which best illustrates the many subtleties and stratagems of the game. It is Test cricket which remains the game's showpiece, perhaps to an exaggerated extent. Just as a good Test match may kindle enthusiasm for the game as a whole, so a poor one is denounced as being to the game's discredit, though a root cause may have been unhelpful weather or a lifeless pitch.

TEST MATCH RECORDS

Australia have won slightly more of their 251 Test matches with England, 95 against England's 83. Of those 251 matches many have become pieces of history readily recalled, such as that at The Oval in 1902 when, after Gilbert Jessop had hit 104 in 75 minutes, the last pair, the Yorkshiremen Hirst and Rhodes, scored the final 15 runs for England to win by one wicket. After the First World War Australia won eight Tests in a row. But England recovered the Ashes in a memorable match at The Oval in 1926 when Hobbs and Sutcliffe made 100s on a wet pitch and Australia were bowled out by the 21-year-old Harold Larwood and Wilfred Rhodes aged 48.

England won the 1928-29 series in Australia and then the so-called 'Bodyline' series of 1932-33. The England captain, Douglas Jardine, instructed those of his fast bowlers who would do so to direct their bowling at the batsman's body with an arc of close fielders on the leg side. It was a move originally designed to counter the brilliantly prolific Australian batsman Don Bradman, then in his heyday, and it led to a bitterness which marred England-Australian relations for some years. Though short-pitched bowling has played a major part in later series, as when Lillee and Thomson bowled on fast, sometimes untrue, pitches in the 1970s, the Bodyline series remains one of the least happy pieces of cricket history.

Acrimony had receded by the time the last England-Australia Test of the inter-war period was played and Len Hutton, batting for 13 hours 20 minutes, made the 364 which is still the highest of the long series and the second highest in Test history. After the Second World War Australia were again on top and in 1948 Bradman led one of their best sides to England. If he had scored four runs in his last innings at The Oval, he would have averaged 100 in Test cricket. No other batsman has exceeded 60.

After the retirement of Bradman, England began to recover, regained the Ashes in 1953 and held them in a successful series in Australia in 1954-55, largely through the fast bowling of Frank Tyson and the batting of the youthful Peter May and Colin Cowdrey. An Australian decline towards the end of the 1960s was followed by an upsurge with the fast bowling of Lillee and Thomson in the 1970s. But by then the supremacy of

TEST CRICKET

both countries had been undermined by the brilliant batting and fast bowling of West Indies.

West Indies had gathered strength during the Second World War when top class cricket was still played in the Caribbean and players of the calibre of Worrell, Weekes and Walcott had emerged. They won a series in England for the first time in 1950 and though they were not always at their best in Australia and it was not until 1979-80 that they won a series there, they took part in the most exhilarating series of all in 1960-61. The First Test at Brisbane was tied, off the seventh ball of the last possible over—the only tie in Test history—and the series ended 2-1 to Australia with crowds of up to 90,000 packing the Melbourne Cricket Ground to watch the final Test.

South Africa won their first Test match in England in 1935 and their first series there 30 years later. Once in the 1950s and once in the 1960s they went to Australia with little hope and, helped by the brilliant fielding of young sides, emerged with a drawn series. Though they had often done well against England at home, they did not win a Test match against Australia in South Africa until December 1964 but they won that series 3-1 and routed Australia three years later.

India's strength on their own slow pitches was in contrast with their struggles in overseas conditions. Their victory at The Oval in 1971, which gave them the series, is still the only Test match they have won in England. A few months before, they had also won a series in West Indies for the only time. They did not win a match in Australia until the late 1970s.

This reflected the slow progress of the newer Test-playing countries towards maintaining consistently high standards. New Zealand did not win a Test match until they beat West Indies 26 years after their first Test. Their first Test win over England was at Wellington in a halved series in 1977-78 and their first win in England, that at Headingley in 1983.

Pakistan, by contrast, made an unexpected impact on their first visit to England in 1954. Having been largely outplayed for much of a rain-affected series, they found conditions suiting their fast-medium bowlers at The Oval in the last Test and won a victory which enabled them to halve the series. But though increasingly hard to beat at home and able to provide tough opposition in Australia and in West Indies, they did not win another Test in England until 1982 when rather unluckily they lost a close series 2-1.

In the later 1970s international cricket entered a period of commercialism which moved the atmosphere of Test cricket even more sharply away from its leisurely beginnings. But, before that, a Centenary Match was played in Melbourne with an extraordinary result. Exactly 100 years to the day after Australia had beaten England in the first Test, they won again—and by the identical margin of 45 runs.

TEST CRICKET RECORDS

SUMMARY OF ALL TEST MATCHES 1876-77 to 1983 †

		Tests	Won by E	A	SA
England	v Australia	251	83	95	-
	v South Africa	102	46	-	18
	v West Indies	80	21	-	-
	v New Zealand	57	30	-	-
	v India	67	28	-	-
	v Pakistan	36	13	-	-
	v Sri Lanka	1	1	-	-
Australia	v South Africa	53	-	29	11
	v West Indies	52	-	26	-
	v New Zealand	15	-	8	-
	v India	39	-	20	-
	v Pakistan	23	-	9	-
	v Sri Lanka	1	-	1	-
South Africa	v New Zealand	17	-	-	9
West Indies	v New Zealand	17	-	-	-
	v India	48	-	-	-
	v Pakistan	19	-	-	-
New Zealand	v India	25	-	-	-
	v Pakistan	21	-	-	-
	v Sri Lanka	2	-	-	-
India	v Pakistan	30	-	-	-
	v Sri Lanka	1	-	-	-
Pakistan	v Sri Lanka	3	-	-	-
Totals		960	222	188	38

	Tests	Won	Lost	Drawn	Tied	Toss Won
England	594	222	150	222	-	294
Australia	434	188	125	120	1	220
South Africa	172	38	77	57	-	80
West Indies	216	69	59	87	1	116
New Zealand	154	16	70	68	-	72
India	210	35	77	98	-	101
Pakistan	132	30	34	68	-	73
Sri Lanka	8	-	6	2	-	4

† up to and including 13 September 1983

WI	NZ	I	P	SL	Tied	Drawn
-	-	-	-	-	-	73
-	-	-	-	-	-	38
25	-	-	-	-	-	34
-	2	-	-	-	-	25
-	-	8	-	-	-	31
-	-	-	2	-	-	21
-	-	-	-	-	-	-
-	-	-	-	-	-	13
13	-	-	-	-	1	12
-	2	-	-	-	-	5
-	-	8	-	-	-	11
-	-	-	8	-	-	6
-	-	-	-	-	-	-
-	2	-	-	-	-	6
5	3	-	-	-	-	9
19	-	5	-	-	-	24
7	-	-	4	-	-	8
-	4	10	-	-	-	11
-	1	-	8	-	-	12
-	2	-	-	-	-	-
-	-	4	6	-	-	20
-	-	-	-	-	-	1
-	-	-	2	-	-	1
69	16	35	30	-	1	361

Key To Abbreviations

- **A** Australia
- **E** England
- **I** India
- **NZ** New Zealand
- **P** Pakistan
- **SA** South Africa
- **SL** Sri Lanka
- **WI** West Indies
- ***** not out

Imran Khan, Pakistan's captain and one of the world's leading all-round cricketers.

TEST CRICKET RECORDS

TEAM RECORDS

Highest Totals By Each Country

	Total	Opponents	Venue	Series
England	903-7d	Australia	The Oval	1938
Australia	758-8d	West Indies	Kingston	1954-55
South Africa	622-9d	Australia	Durban	1969-70
West Indies	790-3d	Pakistan	Kingston	1957-58
New Zealand	551-9d	England	Lord's	1973
India	644-7d	West Indies	Kanpur	1978-79
Pakistan	*657-8d	West Indies	Bridgetown	1957-58
Sri Lanka	454	Pakistan	Faisalabad	1981-82

* Highest total in the second innings of any Test match, highest total by a side following on in Test cricket, and the longest innings (16hr 50min) in all first-class cricket.

Highest Fourth Innings Totals

To Win:	406-4	I v WI	Port-of-Spain	1975-76
To Draw:	654-5	E v SA	Durban	1938-39
To Lose:	445	I v A	Adelaide	1977-78

Highest Match Aggregate

1981	South Africa v England	Durban	1938-39

Largest Margin of Victory

Innings and 579 runs	E v A	The Oval	1938

Longest Match

43 hr 16 min	SA v E	Durban	1938-39

Most Runs In One Day

588	England (398-6) v India (190-0)	Manchester	1936

Lowest Innings Totals By Each Country

	Total	Opponents	Venue	Series
England	45	Australia	Sydney	1886-87
Australia	36	England	Birmingham	1902
South Africa	30 30	England England	Pt Elizabeth Birmingham	1895-96 1924
West Indies	76	Pakistan	Dacca	1958-59

TEST CRICKET RECORDS

New Zealand	26	England	Auckland	1954-55
India	42	England	Lord's	1974
Pakistan	62	Australia	Perth	1981-82
Sri Lanka	93	New Zealand	Wellington	1982-83

Lowest Match Aggregate (Completed Match)

234   Australia v South Africa   Melbourne   1931-32

Side Dismissed Twice In One Day

India (58 and 82) v England   Manchester   1952

Shortest Match

5 hr 53 min   A v SA   Melbourne   1931-32

Smallest Margins of Victory

1 wkt: six instances by England (3), Australia, South Africa and New Zealand.

3 runs: Australia beat England   Manchester   1902
            England beat Australia   Melbourne   1982-83

Tied Test Match

Australia v West Indies   Brisbane   1960-61

Victory Off Last Possible Ball

England beat South Africa (2 wkts)   Durban   1948-49

Fewest Runs Scored in a Full Day's Play

95   Australia (80) v Pakistan (15-2)   Karachi   1956-57

Most Wickets In One Day

27   England (17) v Australia (10)   Lord's   1888

Most Wickets Before Lunch

18   Australia (18) v England   Manchester   1888

Unusual Dismissals

Handled The Ball

WR Endean	SA v E	Cape Town	1956-57
AMJ Hilditch	A v P	Perth	1978-79
Mohsin Khan	P v A	Karachi	1982-83

Obstructing The Field

L Hutton   E v SA   The Oval   1951

TEST CRICKET RECORDS

Run Out By The Bowler
(while backing up before the ball had been bowled)

WA Brown - by MH Mankad	A v I	Sydney	1947-48
IR Redpath - by CC Griffith	A v WI	Adelaide	1968-69
DW Randall - by EJ Chatfield	E v NZ	Christchurch	1977-78
Sikander Bakht - by AG Hurst	P v A	Perth	1978-79

Most Extras In An Innings

68 (B 29, LB 11, NB 28)	P v WI	Bridgetown	1976-77

BATTING RECORDS

3000 RUNS IN TEST

England (20)	Tests	Inn	Not Out	Highest Score	Runs	Average	100s	50s
G Boycott	108	193	23	246*	8114	47.72	22	42
MC Cowdrey	114	188	15	182	7624	44.06	22	38
WR Hammond	85	140	16	336*	7249	58.45	22	24
L Hutton	79	138	15	364	6971	56.67	19	33
KF Barrington	82	131	15	256	6806	58.67	20	35
DCS Compton	78	131	15	278	5807	50.06	17	28
JB Hobbs	61	102	7	211	5410	56.94	15	28
JH Edrich	77	127	9	310*	5138	43.54	12	24
TW Graveney	79	123	13	258	4882	44.38	11	20
H Sutcliffe	54	84	9	194	4555	60.73	16	23
PBH May	66	106	9	285*	4537	46.77	13	22
ER Dexter	62	102	8	205	4502	47.89	9	27
APE Knott	95	149	15	135	4389	32.75	5	30
DI Gower	53	93	8	200*	3742	44.02	7	19
DL Amiss	50	88	10	262*	3612	46.30	11	11
AW Greig	58	93	4	148	3599	40.43	8	20
IT Botham	63	100	3	208	3548	36.57	12	14
EH Hendren	51	83	9	205*	3525	47.63	7	21
FE Woolley	64	98	7	154	3283	36.07	5	23
KWR Fletcher	59	96	14	216	3272	39.90	7	19

Australia (16)	Tests	Inn	Not Out	Highest Score	Runs	Average	100s	50s
DG Bradman	52	80	10	334	6996	99.94	29	13
GS Chappell	82	145	18	247*	6746	53.11	22	31
RN Harvey	79	137	10	205	6149	48.41	21	24
KD Walters	74	125	14	250	5357	48.26	15	33
IM Chappell	75	136	10	196	5345	42.42	14	26

TEST CRICKET RECORDS

	Tests	Inn	Not Out	Highest Score	Runs	Average	100s	50s
WM Lawry	67	123	12	210	5234	47.15	13	27
RB Simpson	62	111	7	311	4869	46.81	10	27
IR Redpath	66	120	11	171	4737	43.45	8	31
KJ Hughes	56	100	6	213	3744	39.82	8	19
RW Marsh	91	144	11	132	3558	26.75	3	16
AR Border	51	91	16	162	3539	47.18	9	21
AR Morris	46	79	3	206	3533	46.48	12	12
C Hill	49	89	2	191	3412	39.21	7	19
VT Trumper	48	89	8	214*	3163	39.04	8	13
CC McDonald	47	83	4	170	3107	39.32	5	17
AL Hassett	43	69	3	198*	3073	46.56	10	11

South Africa (1)	Tests	Inn	Not Out	Highest Score	Runs	Average	100s	50s
B Mitchell	42	80	9	189*	3471	48.88	8	21

West Indies (11)	Tests	Inn	Not Out	Highest Score	Runs	Average	100s	50s
G St A Sobers	93	160	21	365*	8032	57.78	26	30
CH Lloyd	90	149	10	242*	6238	44.87	16	32
RB Kanhai	79	137	6	256	6227	47.53	15	28
E de C Weekes	48	81	5	207	4455	58.61	15	19
IVA Richards	52	80	4	291	4411	58.03	14	19
AI Kallicharran	66	109	10	187	4399	44.43	12	21
RC Fredericks	59	109	7	169	4334	42.49	8	26
FMM Worrell	51	87	9	261	3860	49.48	8	22
CL Walcott	44	74	7	220	3798	56.68	15	14
CC Hunte	44	78	6	260	3245	45.06	8	13
BF Butcher	44	78	6	209*	3104	43.11	7	16

New Zealand (2)	Tests	Inn	Not Out	Highest Score	Runs	Average	100s	50s
BE Congdon	61	114	7	176	3448	32.22	7	19
JR Reid	58	108	5	142	3428	33.28	6	22

India (6)	Tests	Inn	Not Out	Highest Score	Runs	Average	100s	50s
SM Gavaskar	90	158	12	221	7625	52.22	27	33
GR Viswanath	91	155	10	222	6080	41.93	14	35
PR Umrigar	59	94	8	223	3631	42.22	12	14
DB Vengsarkar	63	103	10	157*	3484	37.46	6	20
VL Manjrekar	55	92	10	189*	3208	39.12	7	15
CG Borde	55	97	11	177*	3061	35.59	5	18

TEST CRICKET RECORDS

Pakistan (6)	Tests	Inn	Not Out	Highest Score	Runs	Average	100s	50s
Zaheer Abbas	58	94	7	274	4073	46.81	11	14
Javed Miandad	52	83	14	280*	3992	57.85	10	21
Majid Khan	63	106	5	167	3931	38.92	8	19
Hanif Mohd	55	97	8	337	3915	43.98	12	15
Mushtaq Mohd	57	100	7	201	3643	39.17	10	19
Asif Iqbal	58	99	7	175	3575	38.85	11	12

Sri Lanka (0)

Leading scorer: RL Dias - 543 runs (avge 45.25)

Highest Individual Scores

365*	**G St A Sobers**	WI v P	Kingston	1957-58
364	**L Hutton**	E v A	The Oval	1938
337	**Hanif Mohammad**	P v WI	Bridgetown	1957-58
336*	**WR Hammond**	E v NZ	Auckland	1932-33
334	**DG Bradman**	A v E	Leeds	1930
325	**A Sandham**	E v WI	Kingston	1929-30
311	**RB Simpson**	A v E	Manchester	1964
310*	**JH Edrich**	E v NZ	Leeds	1965
307	**RM Cowper**	A v E	Melbourne	1965-66
304	**DG Bradman**	A v E	Leeds	1934
302	**LG Rowe**	WI v E	Bridgetown	1973-74

The highest individual scores for countries not included above are:

SA	274 RG Pollock	v A	Durban	1969-70
NZ	259 GM Turner	v WI	Georgetown	1971-72
I	231 MH Mankad	v NZ	Madras	1955-56
SL	157 S Wettimuny	v P	Faisalabad	1981-82

Most Runs In A Test Match

380	GS Chappell	A v NZ	Wellington	1973-74

Most Runs In A Series

974	DG Bradman	A v E	1930

Most Runs In A Day

309	DG Bradman	A v E	Leeds	1930

Most Runs Off One Over By One Batsman

24	AME Roberts	WI v E	Port-of-Spain	1980-81

Scored 4,6,2,6,6, leg bye off bowling of IT Botham

24	SM Patil	I v E	Manchester	1982

Scored 4,4,4 (no ball),0,4,4,4 off RGD Willis

TEST CRICKET RECORDS

Most Boundaries In An Innings

57 JH Edrich (310*)　　　　E v NZ　Leeds　　　　1965

Most Sixes In An Innings

10 WR Hammond (336*)　　E v NZ　Auckland　　1932-33

Longest Individual Innings

16 hr 10 min
Hanif Mohammad (337)　　P v WI　Bridgetown　1957-58

Most Hundreds In Test Cricket

29 DG Bradman in 80 innings for Australia
SM Gavaskar equalled this record in his 166th innings
for India, on 29 October 1983

Most Hundreds In A Series

5 CL Walcott for West Indies v Australia　　　　　1954-55

Most Hundreds in Consecutive Innings

5 E de C Weekes for WI v E 1947-48 and v I　　1948-49

Highest Partnerships For Each Wicket (* unbroken)

Wkt	Runs Batsmen	Match	Venue	Series
1st	413 Mankad/Roy	I v NZ	Madras	1955-56
2nd	451 Ponsford/Bradman	A v E	The Oval	1934
3rd	451 Mudassar/Miandad	P v I	Hyderabad	1982-83
4th	411 May/Cowdrey	E v WI	Birmingham	1957
5th	405 Barnes/Bradman	A v E	Sydney	1946-47
6th	346 Fingleton/Bradman	A v E	Melbourne	1936-37
7th	347 Atkinson/Depeiza	WI v A	Bridgetown	1954-55
8th	246 Ames/Allen	E v NZ	Lord's	1931
9th	190 Asif/Intikhab	P v E	The Oval	1967
10th	151 Hastings/Collinge	NZ v P	Auckland	1972-73

BOWLING RECORDS

100 WICKETS IN TESTS

England (26)	T	B	R	W	Avge	Best	5w Inn	10w M
FS Trueman	67	15178	6625	307	21.57	8-31	17	3
RGD Willis	83	16042	7471	305	24.49	8-43	16	-
DL Underwood	86	21862	7674	297	25.83	8-51	17	6
IT Botham	63	14725	6876	277	24.82	8-34	20	4

TEST CRICKET RECORDS

							5w	10w
	T	B	R	W	Avge	Best	Inn	M
JB Statham	70	16056	6261	252	24.84	7-39	9	1
AV Bedser	51	15918	5876	236	24.89	7-34	15	5
JA Snow	49	12021	5387	202	26.66	7-40	8	1
JC Laker	46	12027	4101	193	21.24	10-53	9	3
SF Barnes	27	7873	3106	189	16.43	9-103	24	7
GAR Lock	49	13147	4451	174	25.58	7-35	9	3
MW Tate	39	12523	4055	155	26.16	6-42	7	1
FJ Titmus	53	15118	4931	153	32.22	7-79	7	-
H Verity	40	11173	3510	144	24.37	8-43	5	2
CM Old	46	8858	4020	143	28.11	7-50	4	-
AW Greig	58	9802	4541	141	32.20	8-86	6	2
TE Bailey	61	9712	3856	132	29.21	7-34	5	1
W Rhodes	58	8231	3425	127	26.96	8-68	6	1
DA Allen	39	11297	3779	122	30.97	5-30	4	-
R Illingworth	61	11934	3807	122	31.20	6-29	3	-
J Briggs	33	5332	2094	118	17.74	8-11	9	4
GG Arnold	34	7650	3254	115	28.29	6-45	6	-
GA Lohmann	18	3821	1205	112	10.75	9-28	9	5
DVP Wright	34	8135	4224	108	39.11	7-105	6	1
R Peel	20	5216	1715	102	16.81	7-31	6	2
JH Wardle	28	6597	2080	102	20.39	7-36	5	1
C Blythe	19	4546	1863	100	18.63	8-59	9	4

							5w	10w
Australia (19)	T	B	R	W	Avge	Best	Inn	M
DK Lillee	65	17084	7860	335	23.46	7-83	22	7
R Benaud	63	19108	6704	248	27.03	7-72	16	1
GD McKenzie	60	17681	7328	246	29.78	8-71	16	3
RR Lindwall	61	13650	5251	228	23.03	7-38	12	-
CV Grimmett	37	14513	5231	216	24.21	7-40	21	7
JR Thomson	49	10199	5326	197	27.03	6-46	8	-
AK Davidson	44	11587	3819	186	20.53	7-93	14	2
KR Miller	55	10461	3906	170	22.97	7-60	7	1
WA Johnston	40	11048	3826	160	23.91	6-44	7	-
WJ O'Reilly	27	10024	3254	144	22.59	7-54	11	3
H Trumble	32	8099	3072	141	21.78	8-65	9	3
MHN Walker	34	10094	3792	138	27.47	8-143	6	-
AA Mallett	38	9990	3940	132	29.84	8-59	6	1
B Yardley	33	8909	3986	126	31.63	7-98	6	1
MA Noble	42	7159	3025	121	25.00	7-17	9	2
IW Johnson	45	8780	3182	109	29.19	7-44	3	-
G Giffen	31	6325	2791	103	27.09	7-117	7	1
AN Connolly	29	7818	2981	102	29.22	6-47	4	-
CTB Turner	17	5195	1670	101	16.53	7-43	11	2

							5w	10w
South Africa (4)	T	B	R	W	Avge	Best	Inn	M
HJ Tayfield	37	13568	4405	170	25.91	9-113	14	2
TL Goddard	41	11736	3226	123	26.22	6-53	5	-
PM Pollock	28	6522	2806	116	24.18	6-38	9	1
NAT Adcock	26	6391	2195	104	21.10	6-43	5	-

TEST CRICKET RECORDS

West Indies (10)	T	B	R	W	Avge	Best	5w Inn	10w M
LR Gibbs	79	27115	8989	309	29.09	8-38	18	2
G St A Sobers	93	21599	7999	235	34.03	6-73	6	-
AME Roberts	45	10801	5026	197	25.51	7-54	11	2
WW Hall	48	10421	5066	192	26.38	7-69	9	1
S Ramadhin	43	13939	4579	158	28.98	7-49	10	1
MA Holding	36	8134	3696	151	24.47	8-92	10	2
AL Valentine	36	12953	4215	139	30.32	8-104	8	2
J Garner	32	7326	2861	131	21.83	6-56	2	-
CEH Croft	27	6165	2913	125	23.30	8-29	3	-
VA Holder	40	9095	3627	109	33.27	6-28	3	-

New Zealand (4)	T	B	R	W	Avge	Best	5w Inn	10w M
RJ Hadlee	44	11355	5164	200	25.82	7-23	15	3
RO Collinge	35	7689	3393	116	29.25	6-63	3	-
BR Taylor	30	6334	2953	111	26.60	7-74	4	-
RC Motz	32	7034	3148	100	31.48	6-63	5	-

India (9)	T	B	R	W	Avge	Best	5w Inn	10w M
BS Bedi	67	21364	7637	266	28.71	7-98	14	1
BS Chandrasekhar	58	15963	7199	242	29.74	8-79	16	2
Kapil Dev	53	11572	6082	206	29.52	8-85	15	1
EAS Prasanna	49	14353	5742	189	30.38	8-76	10	2
MH Mankad	44	14686	5236	162	32.32	8-52	8	2
S Venkataraghavan	55	14582	5530	155	35.67	8-72	3	1
SP Gupte	36	11284	4403	149	29.55	9-102	12	1
DR Doshi	32	9202	3450	113	30.53	6-102	5	-
KD Ghavri	39	7042	3656	109	33.54	5-33	4	-

Pakistan (5)	T	B	R	W	Avge	Best	5w Inn	10w M
Imran Khan	49	12552	5318	232	22.92	8-58	16	4
Sarfraz Nawaz	49	12028	5020	155	32.38	9-86	4	1
Fazal Mahmood	34	9834	3434	139	24.70	7-42	13	4
Intikhab Alam	47	10474	4494	125	35.95	7-52	5	2
Iqbal Qasim	36	9294	3426	115	29.79	7-49	4	2

Sri Lanka (0)

Leading wicket-taker: DS de Silva - 27 wickets (avge 35.88)

Record Innings Analyses For Each Country

For	Analysis	Bowler	V	Venue	Series
E	10-53	JC Laker	A	Manchester	1956
A	9-121	AA Mailey	E	Melbourne	1920-21
SA	9-113	HJ Tayfield	E	Johannesburg	1956-57
WI	9-95	JM Noreiga	I	Port-of-Spain	1970-71
NZ	7-23	RJ Hadlee	I	Wellington	1975-76

TEST CRICKET RECORDS

I	9-69	JM Patel	A	Kanpur	1959-60
P	9-86	Sarfraz Nawaz	A	Melbourne	1978-79
SL	5-59	DS de Silva	P	Faisalabad	1981-82

Record Match Analyses For Each Country

For	Analysis	Bowler	V	Venue	Series
E	19-90	JC Laker	A	Manchester	1956
A	16-137	RAL Massie	E	Lord's	1972
SA	13-165	HJ Tayfield	A	Melbourne	1952-53
WI	14-149	MA Holding	E	The Oval	1976
NZ	11-58	RJ Hadlee	I	Wellington	1975-76
I	14-124	JM Patel	A	Kanpur	1959-60
P	14-116	Imran Khan	SL	Lahore	1981-82
SL	9-162	DS de Silva	P	Faisalabad	1981-82

Most Wickets In A Series For Each Country

For	Wickets	Bowler	Opponents	Series
E	49	SF Barnes	South Africa	1913-14
A	44	CV Grimmett	South Africa	1935-36
SA	37	HJ Tayfield	England	1956-57
WI	33	AL Valentine	England	1950
	33	CEH Croft	Pakistan	1976-77
NZ	27	BR Taylor	West Indies	1971-72
I	35	BS Chandrasekhar	England	1972-73
P	40	Imran Khan	India	1982-83
SL	17	DS de Silva	Pakistan	1981-82

Taking The Wickets Of All Eleven Batsmen During A Test

JC Laker	E v A	Manchester	1956
S Venkataraghavan	I v NZ	Delhi	1964-65
G Dymock	A v I	Kanpur	1979-80

Most Wickets By A Bowler In One Day

| 15 | J Briggs | E v SA | Cape Town | 1888-89 |

Four Wickets In Five Balls

| **MJC Allom** | E v NZ | Christchurch | 1929-30 |

On debut and in his eighth over: W-WWW

| **CM Old** | E v I | Birmingham | 1978 |

In the same over: WW-(no ball)WW

Hat-Tricks

There have been 17 hat-tricks (three wickets with consecutive balls by the same bowler within one match) in Test cricket. Two bowlers have achieved this feat twice:

H Trumble	A v E	Melbourne	1901-02
	A v E	Melbourne	1903-04
TJ Matthews (2)	A v SA	Manchester	1912

Took a hat-trick in each innings and on the same afternoon

TEST CRICKET RECORDS

Hat-Tricks Since 1946

PJ Loader	E v WI	Leeds	1957
LF Kline	A v SA	Cape Town	1957-58
WW Hall	WI v P	Lahore	1958-59
GM Griffin	SA v E	Lord's	1960
LR Gibbs	WI v A	Adelaide	1960-61
PJ Petherick †	NZ v P	Lahore	1976-77

† On Test debut

Most Runs Conceded In An Innings

298	LO Fleetwood-Smith A v E	The Oval	1938

Most Runs Conceded In A Match

374	OC Scott WI v E	Kingston	1929-30

Most Balls Bowled In An Innings

588	S Ramadhin WI v E	Birmingham	1957

Most Balls Bowled In A Match

774	S Ramadhin WI v E	Birmingham	1957

WICKET-KEEPING RECORDS

100 Dismissals In Tests

	For	Tests	Dis	Ct	St
RW Marsh	A	91	334	322	12
APE Knott	E	95	269	250	19
TG Evans	E	91	219	173	46
Wasim Bari	P	73	201	175	26
DL Murray	WI	62	189	181	8
ATW Grout	A	51	187	163	24
RW Taylor	E	51	162	155	7
SMH Kirmani	I	69	160	128	32
JHB Waite	SA	50	141	124	17
WAS Oldfield	A	54	130	78	52
JM Parks	E	46	114	103	11

The records for New Zealand and Sri Lanka are:

KJ Wadsworth	NZ	33	96	92	4
HM Goonatillake	SL	5	13	10	3

Most Dismissals In An Innings

7 (all ct) Wasim Bari	P v NZ	Auckland	1978-79
7 (all ct) RW Taylor	E v I	Bombay	1979-80

TEST CRICKET RECORDS

Most Dismissals In A Match

| 10 (all ct) RW Taylor | E v I | Bombay | 1979-80 |

Most Dismissals In A Series

| 28 (all ct) RW Marsh | Australia v England | 1982-83 |

Highest Innings Totals In Which No Byes Were Conceded

| 659-8d | TG Evans | E v A | Sydney | 1946-47 |
| 652 | SMH Kirmani | I v P | Faisalabad | 1982-83 |

FIELDING RECORDS

100 Catches In Tests

	For	Tests	Catches
MC Cowdrey	England	114	120
GS Chappell	Australia	82	114
RB Simpson	Australia	62	110
WR Hammond	England	85	110
G St A Sobers	West Indies	93	109
IM Chappell	Australia	75	105

The records for the other countries are:

South Africa	B Mitchell	42	56
New Zealand	BE Congdon	61	44
India	SM Gavaskar	90	80
Pakistan	Majid Khan	63	70
Sri Lanka	Y Goonasekera	2	6

Most Catches In An Innings

| 5 | VY Richardson | A v SA | Durban | 1935-36 |
| 5 | Yajurvindra Singh | I v E | Bangalore | 1976-77 |

Greg Chappell surpassed Colin Cowdrey's catching record in his last Test, in January 1984, taking his aggregate to 122.

TEST CRICKET RECORDS

Most Catches In A Match

7 GS Chappell	A v E	Perth	1974-75
7 Yajurvindra Singh	I v E	Bangalore	1976-77

Most Catches In A Series

15 JM Gregory	Australia v England	1920-21

ALL-ROUND RECORDS

1000 Runs And 100 Wickets In Tests

England	Tests	Runs	Wickets	Tests for Double
TE Bailey	61	2290	132	47
IT Botham	63	3548	277	21
AW Greig	58	3599	141	37
R Illingworth	61	1836	122	47
W Rhodes	58	2325	127	44
MW Tate	39	1198	155	33
FJ Titmus	53	1449	153	40

Australia	Tests	Runs	Wickets	Tests for Double
R Benaud	63	2201	248	32
AK Davidson	44	1328	186	34
G Giffen	31	1238	103	30
IW Johnson	45	1000	109	45
RR Lindwall	61	1502	228	38
KR Miller	55	2958	170	33
MA Noble	42	1997	121	27

South Africa	Tests	Runs	Wickets	Tests for Double
TL Goddard	41	2516	123	36

West Indies	Tests	Runs	Wickets	Tests for Double
G St A Sobers	93	8032	235	48

Sobers also held 109 catches

New Zealand	Tests	Runs	Wickets	Tests for Double
RJ Hadlee	44	1601	200	28

India	Tests	Runs	Wickets	Tests for Double
Kapil Dev	53	2253	206	25
MH Mankad	44	2109	162	23

TEST CRICKET RECORDS

Pakistan

Imran Khan	49	1853	232	30
Intikhab Alam	47	1493	125	41

100 Runs And 10 Wickets In A Match

AK Davidson	44 / 80	5-135 / 6-87	A v WI	Brisbane	1960-61
IT Botham	114	6-58 / 7-48	E v I	Bombay	1979-80
Imran Khan	117	6-98 / 5-82	P v I	Faisalabad	1982-83

300 Runs And 30 Wickets In A Series

	Runs	Wkts			
G Giffen	475	34	A v E		1894-95
R Benaud	329	30	A v SA		1957-58
IT Botham	399	34	E v A		1981

OTHER RECORDS

Most Test Matches As Captain
54   CH Lloyd   West Indies   1974-75 to 1982-83

Most Test Match Appearances
114   MC Cowdrey   England   1954-55 to 1974-75

Most Consecutive Appearances
87   GR Viswanath   India   1970-71 to 1982-83

Youngest Test Cricketer
15y 124d   Mushtaq Mohammad   P v WI   Lahore   1958-59

Oldest Test Cricketer
52y 165d   W Rhodes   E v WI   Kingston   1929-30

Longest Test Career
30y 315d   W Rhodes   England   1899 to 1929-30

Longest Interval Between Appearances
17y 316d   G Gunn   England   1911-12 to 1929-30

Players Who Have Represented Two Countries (Tests)

Amir Elahi	India (1)	Pakistan (5)
JJ Ferris	Australia (8)	England (1)

TEST CRICKET RECORDS

SC Guillen	West Indies (5)	New Zealand (3)
Gul Mahomed	India (8)	Pakistan (1)
F Hearne	England (2)	South Africa (4)
AH Kardar	India (3)	Pakistan (23)
WE Midwinter	Australia (8)	England (4)
F Mitchell	England (2)	South Africa (3)
WL Murdoch	Australia (18)	England (1)
Nawab of Pataudi, sr	England (3)	India (3)
AE Trott	Australia (3)	England (2)
SMJ Woods	Australia (3)	England (3)

CAREER RECORDS OF CURRENT TEST PLAYERS

England	T	R	Av	100s	HS	W	Av	Best	Ct/St
IT Botham	63	3548	36	12	208	277	24	8-34	72
NGB Cook	2	51	12	-	26	17	16	5-35	3
NG Cowans	8	90	7	-	36	23	36	6-77	3
GR Dilley	17	328	16	-	56	45	32	4-24	5
PH Edmonds	23	430	19	-	64	59	29	7-66	23
NA Foster	1	13	6	-	10	1	75	1-35	1
G Fowler	6	436	36	1	105	-	-	-	2
MW Gatting	24	918	23	-	81	-	-	-	21
DI Gower	53	3742	44	7	200*	1	2	1-1	34
AJ Lamb	15	1061	40	3	137*	-	-	-	16
VJ Marks	2	25	8	-	12*	4	27	3-78	-
DW Randall	40	2073	32	5	174	-	-	-	28
CL Smith	2	78	19	-	43	2	15	2-31	2
CJ Tavaré	26	1620	34	2	149	-	-	-	17
RW Taylor	51	1073	17	-	97	-	-	-	155/7
RGD Willis	83	775	11	-	28*	305	24	8-43	37

Australia	T	R	Av	100s	HS	W	Av	Best	Ct/St
AR Border	51	3539	47	9	162	15	34	3-20	58
GS Chappell	82	6746	53	22	247*	47	37	5-61	114
J Dyson	27	1282	28	2	127*	-	-	-	10
TG Hogan	1	-	-	-	-	6	19	5-66	1
RM Hogg	26	272	8	-	36	94	24	6-74	5
DW Hookes	14	923	41	1	143*	-	-	-	6
KJ Hughes	56	3744	39	8	213	-	-	-	40
GF Lawson	13	245	13	-	57*	59	23	7-81	3
DK Lillee	65	874	13	-	73*	335	23	7-83	21
RW Marsh	91	3558	26	3	132	-	-	-	322/12
CG Rackemann	1	4	4	-	4	2	48	2-61	1
JR Thomson	49	641	12	-	49	197	27	6-46	19
KC Wessels	5	527	58	2	162	-	-	-	8

TEST CRICKET RECORDS

GM Wood	42	2554	33	7	126	-	-	-	32
RD Woolley	1	-	-	-	-	-	-	-	5
GN Yallop	33	2199	37	6	172	1	116	1-21	17

West Indies	T	R	Av	100s	HS	W	Av	Best	Ct/St
WW Daniel	5	29	9	-	11	15	25	4-53	2
WW Davis	1	14	14	-	14	4	43	2-54	1
PJ Dujon	8	486	48	1	110	-	-	-	27/1
J Garner	32	424	12	-	60	131	21	6-56	26
HA Gomes	27	1596	42	5	126	8	58	2-20	7
CG Greenidge	41	2962	45	6	154*	-	-	-	43
DL Haynes	29	1764	41	4	184	1	8	1-2	17
MA Holding	36	461	11	-	58*	151	24	8-92	12
CH Lloyd	90	6238	44	16	242*	10	62	2-13	68
AL Logie	5	167	27	1	130	-	-	-	1
MD Marshall	17	200	10	-	45	55	28	5-37	7
IVA Richards	52	4411	58	14	291	14	56	2-19	56
AME Roberts	45	694	13	-	54	197	25	7-54	9

New Zealand	T	R	Av	100s	HS	W	Av	Best	Ct/St
JC Bracewell	8	85	7	-	28	21	31	5-75	6
BL Cairns	32	739	16	-	52*	97	31	7-74	23
EJ Chatfield	10	60	8	-	13*	29	37	5-95	-
JV Coney	24	1146	31	-	84	15	32	3-28	28
JJ Crowe	4	81	11	-	36	-	-	-	3
MD Crowe	7	183	15	-	46	2	36	2-35	8
BA Edgar	24	1481	36	3	161	-	-	-	13
TJ Franklin	1	9	4	-	7	-	-	-	-
EJ Gray	2	38	9	-	17	4	32	3-73	-
RJ Hadlee	44	1601	24	1	103	200	25	7-23	22
GP Howarth	34	2014	35	6	147	3	78	1-13	22
WK Lees	21	778	23	1	152	-	-	-	52/7
IDS Smith	9	108	10	-	20	-	-	-	29
MC Snedden	9	120	15	-	32	23	30	3-21	2
GM Turner	41	2991	44	7	259	-	-	-	42
JG Wright	25	1233	28	2	141	-	-	-	12

India	T	R	Av	100s	HS	W	Av	Best	Ct/St
M Amarnath	37	2648	44	7	120	26	56	4-63	32
KBJ Azad	4	107	17	-	24	1	158	1-35	2
RMH Binny	9	198	15	-	46	15	42	3-53	7
DR Doshi	32	129	4	-	20	113	30	6-102	10
AD Gaekwad	26	1289	29	1	102	-	-	-	8
SM Gavaskar	90	7625	52	27	221	1	173	1-34	80
Kapil Dev	53	2253	32	3	126*	206	29	8-85	19
SMH Kirmani	69	2100	24	1	101*	-	-	-	128/32
Madan Lal	31	762	20	-	55*	64	36	5-23	14
SM Patil	20	1254	43	3	174	9	26	2-28	8
BS Sandhu	7	206	34	-	71	9	53	3-87	1

TEST CRICKET RECORDS

	T	R	Av	100s	HS	W	Av	Best	Ct/St
RJ Shastri	19	669	30	2	128	42	39	5-125	8
K Srikkanth	6	147	16	-	65	-	-	-	2
DB Vengsarkar	63	3484	37	6	157*	-	-	-	44
S Venkataraghavan	55	737	11	-	64	155	35	8-72	44
Y Sharma	33	1650	39	2	140	1	7	1-6	13

Pakistan	T	R	Av	100s	HS	W	Av	Best	Ct/St
Abdul Qadir	19	255	14	-	38	65	33	7-142	6
Imran Khan	49	1853	29	2	123	232	22	8-58	16
Iqbal Qasim	36	269	9	-	56	115	29	7-49	27
Javed Miandad	52	3992	57	10	280*	17	37	3-74	48/1
Mansoor Akhtar	13	484	25	1	111	-	-	-	7
Mohammad Nazir	8	89	22	-	29*	26	24	7-99	2
Mohsin Khan	22	1516	48	4	200	-	-	-	18
Mudassar Nazar	35	2138	43	6	231	25	33	6-32	23
Salim Malik	8	261	37	2	107	-	-	-	9
Sarfraz Nawaz	49	827	15	-	55	155	32	9-86	25
Tahir Naqqash	10	182	22	-	57	23	39	5-40	1
Wasim Bari	73	1259	16	-	85	-	-	-	175/26
Wasim Raja	45	2321	37	2	117*	39	36	4-68	12
Zaheer Abbas	58	4073	46	11	274	-	-	-	31

Sri Lanka	T	R	Av	100s	HS	W	Av	Best	Ct/St
RG de Alwis	2	15	3	-	9	-	-	-	1
ALF de Mel	6	154	15	-	34	25	36	5-68	5
DS de Silva	8	364	26	-	61	27	35	5-59	3
RL Dias	6	543	45	1	109	-	-	-	3
ERNS Fernando	3	73		-	46	-	-	-	-
Y Goonasekera	2	48	12	-	23	-	-	-	6
RPW Guneratne	1	0	0	-	0*	-	-	-	-
S Jeganathan	2	19	4	-	8	-	-	-	-
VB John	2	11	5	-	8*	8	17	5-60	1
RS Madugalle	8	431	28	-	91*	-	-	-	5
LRD Mendis	6	450	37	2	105	-	-	-	4
A Ranatunga	5	266	26	-	90	1	84	1-72	1
RJ Ratnayake	3	58	9	-	30	7	51	4-81	1
JR Ratnayeke	5	102	12	-	29*	9	50	3-93	-
SAR Silva	1	8	4	-	8	-	-	-	2
M de S Wettimuny	2	28	7	-	17	-	-	-	2
S Wettimuny	7	514	39	1	157	-	-	-	3

* denotes not out

Statistics exclude matches played after 13 September 1983

GREAT CRICKETERS

Statistics exclude matches played after 13 September 1983
* denotes not out

SYDNEY FRANCIS BARNES

(1873-1967)

Sydney Barnes, sometimes called the greatest bowler of all time, had an unusual career in that for most of the years between 1901 and 1914 when he was playing in Test matches, the England selectors were picking him on his form in League and Minor County cricket. He played a few matches for Warwickshire in the mid-1890s and for Lancashire throughout 1902 and 1903 but between 1904 and 1934 he played for Staffordshire, taking 1432 wickets for them.

A tall upright figure, he bowled with a springy run-up at above medium pace. His high arm and long strong fingers gave him great control and allowed him to swing the ball and move it either way off the pitch. He was effective on good pitches where others were innocuous and his record in Australia and South Africa was astonishing.

He began one Test match in Melbourne in 1911-12 by taking four Australian wickets in five overs for one run. Two years later in Johannesburg he took 17 South African wickets for 159, a feat only surpassed in first-class cricket when Jim Laker took his 19 wickets in the Old Trafford Test of 1956. In that 1913-14 series Barnes took a record 49 wickets in four Tests. Illness kept him out of the Fifth and though he was to live to 94, he suffered ill-health during several periods of his playing career. Yet his skill and the economy of his action were such that he played League cricket until he was 61 and took 86 wickets in the year of his retirement, 1934.

FIRST-CLASS CAREER (1894-1930)

Inns	NO	HS	Runs	Avge	100s
173	50	93	1573	12.78	-

Wkts	Avge	Best	5 Wkts	Ct
719	17.09	9-103	68	65

TEST MATCHES (27)

Inns	NO	HS	Runs	Avge	100s
39	9	38*	242	8.06	-

Wkts	Avge	Best	5 Wkts	Ct
189	16.43	9-103	24	12

ALEC VICTOR BEDSER
(1918-   )

Though Alec Bedser, like his twin brother Eric, lost some of his best years as a player through the Second World War, he was for seven years afterwards England's leading bowler. His Test career ended in 1955 but he played for Surrey until 1960, captaining them in that season in the absence, through illness, of Peter May.

A successful businessman, he still made time after his retirement to serve on committees and to begin in 1962 a period of over 20 years as a selector. For 13 years from 1969 he was chairman of selectors. He was assistant-manager to the Duke of Norfolk on the MCC tour of Australia and New Zealand in 1962-63 and twice managed England teams to Australia in the 1970s.

Tall and powerfully built, he had a bowling action which was a marvel of economy with a short run-up and a swing of the massive body which dragged the maximum bounce from the pitch and yet allowed him to sustain life and accuracy at a fast-medium pace over long periods.

He bowled mainly the inswinger with which he had many illustrious opponents, from Don Bradman downwards, caught at backward short-leg. But he also bowled a slightly slower leg-cutter which on a wet pitch would be akin to a fast high-bouncing leg-break to which few batsmen could be expected to have an answer.

If he had not been so heavily employed as a bowler, he would have made more runs, for as a batsman he was a good timer of the ball and played very straight.

FIRST-CLASS CAREER (1939-60)

Inns	NO	HS	Runs	Avge	100s
567	181	126	5735	14.51	1

Wkts	Avge	Best	5 Wkts	Ct
1924	20.41	8-18	96	289

TEST MATCHES (51)

Inns	NO	HS	Runs	Avge	100s
71	15	79	714	12.75	-

Wkts	Avge	Best	5 Wkts	Ct
236	24.89	7-34	15	26

IAN TERRENCE BOTHAM
(1955-)

Ian Botham, already powerfully built when he first played for Somerset in 1973 aged 17, took barely five years to become England's leading all-rounder. Within two more he was breaking countless records, as with the innings of 114 and the 13 wickets for 106 runs in a Bombay Test against India in 1980. It is sometimes said that his figures are flattering because of the modern proliferation of Test matches and of the relatively modest nature of the opposition in some series. But the belligerent, often spectacular, manner in which he has made his runs and the consistency with which he has taken his wickets are unquestionable.

His innings of 149 not out against Australia at Headingley in 1981, begun when England were in imminent danger of an innings defeat, enabled them to bring off a historic victory. As if this was not enough, he took five wickets for one run to win another close victory in the next Test at Edgbaston and in the next at Old Trafford played a devastating innings of 118, making the last 90 out of 103 in 13½ overs and 55 minutes.

Immensely strong, he is a fine sight as a batsman with bat swinging in a full arc. As a fast-medium bowler, he is not always accurate but at best is capable of swinging the ball a lot and beating the best of batsmen. He has taken many brilliant slip catches and has the inexplicable gift of seldom being out of the action in a match.

As England captain for just over a year from June 1980, he had a difficult time in two series against the powerful West Indies and this period corresponded, whether by coincidence or not, with one of his rare losses of form.

FIRST-CLASS CAREER (1974-)

Inns	NO	HS	Runs	Avge	100s
351	25	228	10701	32.82	23

Wkts	Avge	Best	5 Wkts	Ct
777	25.00	8-34	44	214

TEST MATCHES (63)

Inns	NO	HS	Runs	Avge	100s
100	3	208	3548	36.57	12

Wkts	Avge	Best	5 Wkts	Ct
277	24.82	8-34	20	72

GREAT CRICKETERS

GEOFFREY BOYCOTT
(1940-)

Geoffrey Boycott's long career as a highly productive batsman has been tinged by sadness, for his dedication to batting and his painstaking effort to banish error and make 100 per cent of his opportunities have brought claims that he puts his own runs before his side's interests.

His critics may say with some justification that he has often prospered when the side has not and that though he has saved many matches, he has not won many. To this he would answer, not at times without truth, that he always carried the major burden of his side's batting and he can certainly point to the Trinidad Test of 1974 as one which England would certainly not have won without his 99 and 112.

He captained Yorkshire in the 1970s for eight seasons which were not successful ones. No one can say whether they would have been any more successful under another captain.

During this period his complex personality led him to withdraw from Test cricket for three years. As this coincided with a period in which England were battered in two series by the fierce fast bowling of Lillee and Thomson, Boycott was bound to suffer criticism that his absence and the rise of formidable Australian fast bowlers were not unconnected.

Yet he was a fine player of the fastest bowling, as well as a masterly player of spin and a more fluent and versatile strokeplayer than he usually allowed himself to look.

A model cricketer in his neatness of dress, he is an accurate bowler swinging the ball at medium pace and has made himself into a highly efficient fielder, perhaps the most unfailingly accurate thrower from the deep of his time.

FIRST-CLASS CAREER (1962-)

Inns	NO	HS	Runs	Avge	100s
925	139	261*	44210	56.24	139

Wkts	Avge	Best	5 Wkts	Ct
45	31.22	4-14	-	237

TEST MATCHES (108)

Inns	NO	HS	Runs	Avge	100s
193	23	246*	8114	47.72	22

Wkts	Avge	Best	5 Wkts	Ct
7	54.57	3-47	-	33

GREAT CRICKETERS

SIR DONALD GEORGE BRADMAN
(1908-)

For those who saw him in his prime before the Second World War there has never been a batsman to rival Don Bradman. The speed, certainty and judgment with which he made his runs were remarkable but so were the quantity and the consistency with which they were made. He was so dominant, even at the highest level, that if on a reasonably good pitch he did not make a hundred, he was almost considered to have failed. He made a hundred for every 2.88 times that he went to the wicket. Even the great Jack Hobbs only averaged a hundred in every 6.67 innings.

From his first Sheffield Shield match for New South Wales in 1927 and his first Test a year later Bradman revealed an unusually early sight of the ball and lightning reflexes. Of no more than medium height and of slight build, he had a gift of timing which, added to the fact that he always seemed to be in position waiting for the ball, sent it racing through the gaps in the field, seldom it seemed, off the ground. He found opportunities to score where others did not, he had the confidence and skill to dominate all types of bowling and the temperament to want to go on batting, however many runs he had made. It may have been clinical in its efficiency but it was inventive, inspiring and a privilege to watch.

Of so many brilliant feats up to his final tour of England in 1948, many will choose his 254 at Lord's in 1930 as an innings of sheer perfection. His 334 at Leeds, a fortnight later, included a record 309 runs on the first day. His first two innings in England that year, aged 21, had been 236 and 185 not out. From 1936-37 he captained Australia and after his retirement served Australian cricket for many years as administrator, selector and shrewd adviser.

FIRST-CLASS CAREER (1927/8-1948/9)

Inns	NO	HS	Runs	Avge	100s
338	43	452*	28067	95.14	117

Wkts	Avge	Best	5 Wkts	Ct St
36	37.97	3-35	-	131 1

TEST MATCHES (52)

Inns	NO	HS	Runs	Avge	100s
80	10	334	6996	99.94	29

Wkts	Avge	Best	5 Wkts	Ct
2	36.00	1-8	-	32

GREGORY STEPHEN CHAPPELL

(1948-)

Greg Chappell is a far more technically correct and more polished batsman than his successful brother, Ian, his predecessor as Australian captain. His talent was recognised in England as early as 1968 and 1969 when he spent two seasons playing for Somerset. By 1970-71 he was in the Australian Test side and it was not long before he was sustaining the Australian innings not only consistently and productively but with an elegance all his own among modern Australian batsmen. His effortless, sweetly timed on-drive was always a joy to watch.

He moved from South Australia to Queensland as captain in 1973-74 and though there have been times when he looked drained by Test cricket and in less than robust health, he was seldom out of form for long.

In the late 1970s, which included the World Series seasons, he was, like most of the leading Australians, out of first-class cricket. He had become captain of Australia in 1975-76 but was soon finding the strain of touring too much for him. He went to Pakistan in 1979-80 but not to India a year later nor to England in 1981. He was always missed, for in his generation he was a class above the other Australian batsmen.

FIRST-CLASS CAREER (1966/7-)

Inns	NO	HS	Runs	Avge	100s
520	68	247*	23581	52.17	71

Wkts	Avge	Best	5 Wkts	Ct
286	28.86	7-40	5	357

TEST MATCHES (82)

Inns	NO	HS	Runs	Avge	100s
145	18	247*	6746	53.11	22

Wkts	Avge	Best	5 Wkts	Ct
47	37.40	5-61	1	114

Editor's note: Chappell announced his retirement from Test cricket before the last Test in the 1983-84 home series with Pakistan. His 182 runs in the last Test took his aggregate to 7,110 (average 53.86), beating Bradman's Australian record in Tests. And his 3 catches took his Test tally to 122, surpassing Colin Cowdrey's world record.

GREAT CRICKETERS

DENIS CHARLES SCOTT COMPTON
(1918-   )

Denis Compton's special place among the great batsmen of cricket history is undisputed. If the Second World War had not taken six years out of his career in his 20s, if he had not been handicapped for over half his playing career by a knee injury and if he had been more conscious of feats and figures, his record would have been even more remarkable than it was.

But it is for the character and entertainment of his batting that he is remembered even more than for its quality. He had the gift of communicating to the spectator his feelings about the bowling, whether confident or concerned. This with the fluency and inventiveness of his strokeplay based on a sound technique made him fascinating to watch. He was also a colourful and often effective left-arm spinner of the chinaman and googly. And on the football field he won a Cupwinner's medal with Arsenal in 1950.

When he was just 18 in 1936 he played his first match for Middlesex, batting number eleven. Within a month he had made the first of his 123 first-class hundreds and a year later was playing in his first Test match.

In his first Test match against Australia he made 102 and after his golden year of 1947 when his 3816 runs and 18 100s set records unlikely to be beaten, he played two more memorable innings against Bradman's unbeaten Australians in 1948—184 at Trent Bridge and 145 not out, after retiring hurt with a head injury early on, at Old Trafford. Though frequently interrupted by the need for repairs to his knee, including the removal of the knee-cap, he came back to play brilliant innings, including 158 against South Africa in 1955 and 94 against Australia in 1956. But that winter's tour of South Africa was his last and after the 1957 season he retired.

FIRST-CLASS CAREER (1936-64)

Inns	NO	HS	Runs	Avge	100s
839	88	300	38942	51.85	123

Wkts	Avge	Best	5 Wkts	Ct
622	32.27	7-36	20	416

TEST MATCHES (78)

Inns	NO	HS	Runs	Avge	100s
131	15	278	5807	50.06	17

Wkts	Avge	Best	5 Wkts	Ct
25	56.40	5-70	1	49

MICHAEL COLIN COWDREY
(1932-)

A gifted games-player, Colin Cowdrey, though heavily built, was amazingly quick in his reactions, a gift demonstrated by his slip-catching as well as by his batting. He was only 21 when he began his Test career in Australia in 1954-55, having first played for Kent in 1950. He had already proved his quality by being relatively more effective against better bowling and in only his second Test he shared in a partnership with Peter May which turned the match—and indeed the series—in England's favour. In the next Test his remarkable 102 out of a total of only 191 started England on the way to another victory.

Though he was to play in 114 Tests and make 22 Test 100s, his subsequent career never quite became the uninterrupted success which had seemed likely from such a start. Partly perhaps he was affected by having to fill in as an opening batsman when he would rather have batted further down the order, partly perhaps his coming and going from the England captaincy had its effect and undermined his belief in himself. It was no help to his confidence to send him four times to Australia as vice-captain under different captains, though he led England to an unexpected victory in West Indies in 1967-68.

He captained Kent from 1957 for 15 years but many of his finest innings were played overseas where faster pitches made his reliance on timing rather than power more effective. At his best he played majestically and on a level only the most talented attain and it was his technique against fast bowling which led England to send for him in an emergency in 1974-75. Thus at 42 he went to Australia on his sixth and last tour.

FIRST-CLASS CAREER (1950-76)

Inns	NO	HS	Runs	Avge	100s
1130	134	307	42719	42.89	107

Wkts	Avge	Best	5 Wkts	Ct
65	51.21	4-22	-	638

TEST MATCHES (114)

Inns	NO	HS	Runs	Avge	100s
188	15	182	7624	44.06	22

Wkts	Avge	Best	5 Wkts	Ct
-	-	-	-	120

GREAT CRICKETERS

SUNIL MANOHAR GAVASKAR
(1949-)

Though Sunil Gavaskar was the mainstay of the Indian batting throughout the 1970s, during which he made 100s against all the Test-playing countries (no less than 10 against West Indies) and broke many records, his first Test series was in some ways the most remarkable. India were given little chance of winning in the Caribbean in 1970-71. They had never won a Test match against West Indies in five previous series but the 21-year-old Gavaskar averaged 154 and, having won the Second Test on a pitch in Trinidad which took spin, they held West Indies to draws in the other matches and won the series. Gavaskar had been unable to play in the First Test through injury but, playing in his first Test, contributed 65 and 67 not out to the victory in Trinidad. In the remaining matches he was only once out for under 100 and in the final Test he scored 124 and 220.

He was less successful in the series which India won in England later in 1971 but it was soon clear that despite his short stature Gavaskar had both the temperament, the sound technique and, as an opening batsman, the opportunity to pose the most obvious threat to date to Sir Donald Bradman's record of 29 Test 100s. So it proved, even though, during a spell as captain of India, his concentration and apparently boundless patience were rather less in evidence than before.

FIRST-CLASS CAREER (1966/7-)

Inns	NO	HS	Runs	Avge	100s
471	49	340	21543	51.04	68

Wkts	Avge	Best	5 Wkts	Ct
21	54.14	3-43	–	251

TEST MATCHES (90)

Inns	NO	HS	Runs	Avge	100s
158	12	221	7625	52.22	27

Wkts	Avge	Best	5 Wkts	Ct
1	173.00	1-34	–	80

Editor's note: During the 1983-84 home Test series with West Indies, Gavaskar scored his 30th Test 100 to beat Bradman's record, and also beat Geoff Boycott's record Test aggregate, taking his total runs in Tests to 8,394.

LANCE GIBBS
(1934-   )

For much of the 1960s Lance Gibbs was one of the best off-spin bowlers in the world, perhaps the best, certainly on hard pitches. He was fortunate to be playing for West Indies at a time when they were seldom short of runs and when their bowling, with such as Hall, Griffith and Sobers in their prime, was varied and penetrative. But tall, willowy and with a quick, supple action, he had a deceptive flight which with a good measure of spin and immaculate control made him especially effective in five-day Tests in dry weather.

Twice on successive West Indies tours to England in 1963 and 1966, he bowled his side to victory at Old Trafford on good pitches which had deteriorated only a little but just enough for him to wear down batsmen facing a big West Indies score. In 1963 he bowled 75.3 overs in the match, taking 11 wickets for 157; in 1966 it was 69.1 overs and 10 for 106.

Gibbs played in league cricket in Lancashire and Durham and qualified to play for Warwickshire in 1968. The less true pitches of county cricket and the quicker tempo of the game made him relatively less effective but he had a prosperous season in 1971 when he bowled more often round the wicket than in the past and took 123 wickets. That almost won Warwickshire the championship, which in fact they did win with a less sizeable contribution from Gibbs a year later. He left Warwickshire in 1973 but was still needed by West Indies in Australia in 1975-76. It was there that 15 years earlier he had performed the first hat-trick against Australia for 61 years and it was there that in his last series he set up a new Test record of 309 wickets.

FIRST-CLASS CAREER (1953/4-1975/6)

Inns	NO	HS	Runs	Avge	100s
352	150	43	1729	8.55	-

Wkts	Avge	Best	5 Wkts	Ct
1024	27.22	8-37	50	203

TEST MATCHES (79)

Inns	NO	HS	Runs	Avge	100s
109	39	25	488	6.97	-

Wkts	Avge	Best	5 Wkts	Ct
309	29.09	8-38	18	52

GREAT CRICKETERS

WILLIAM GILBERT GRACE
(1848-1915)

No one has ever dominated the world of cricket as did Doctor WG Grace for nearly 40 years from the middle of the 1860s. Tall, heavily built and, at an early age, bearded, WG, or 'The Doctor', was not only an all-round cricketer of great skill whose achievements in an unusually long career broke most of the existing records, he was also a man of formidable and striking personality who in his own time became a legend of dictatorial 'gamesmanship' blended with gruff kindliness.

When only just 17 he played for the Gentleman in the big match of the year and he linked the Middle Ages of cricket with the era of the county championship and Test matches. So well did he retain his form that in 1895, in his 47th year, he became the first batsman ever to score 1000 runs in May.

As a batsman he was entirely sound both in judgment of length and in execution of stroke. He was a masterly player of fast bowling, though the pitches of the day were often rough and fiery. His record of 126 hundreds was to stand until 1925.

WG did not qualify as a doctor until he was 31 and there is little doubt that he earned money from cricket and was not the purest amateur. He captained Gloucestershire for the first 29 years of their history and in 1880 opened the innings for England in the first home Test match, with his brother, EM. He made 152. He captained England at home, and on the 1891-92 tour of Australia, until after the first Test of 1899, by which time he was finding his immobility in the field a handicap. In that year he accepted the managership of the new London County Club, a move which sadly brought a break with Gloucestershire. London County perished for financial reasons in 1904 but WG's zest for cricket remained undulled and his last match, for Eltham, was a few days before war broke out.

FIRST-CLASS CAREER (1865-1908)

Inns	NO	HS	Runs	Avge	100s
1478	104	344	54211	39.45	124

Wkts	Avge	Best	5 Wkts	Ct	St
2809	18.13	9-55	239	862	5

TEST MATCHES (22)

Inns	NO	HS	Runs	Avge	100s
36	2	170	1098	32.29	2

Wkts	Avge	Best	5 Wkts	Ct
9	26.22	2-12	-	39

RICHARD JOHN HADLEE
(1951-)

Richard Hadlee, born a few months after his father, Walter, played his last Test match as a much respected captain of New Zealand, had made himself by the late 1970s one of the word's best all-rounders and easily the most successful in New Zealand cricket history.

Wiry in build, he is a fast-medium bowler with an economical run-up, moving the ball enough to unsettle the best of batsmen on occasion and sometimes surprising them with a genuinely fast ball. As an attacking left-handed batsman in the lower middle order, he has restored many a flagging innings with his bold but usually well-judged attack.

He played a major part in New Zealand's first defeat of England at Wellington in 1977-78, taking 10 wickets for 100. His most memorable innings is probably the 81 at Auckland the year before when he came in on a lively pitch against Lillee and a strong Australian bowling side with the score 31 for five.

His value to New Zealand cricket, which usually has no great depth, is immense. Much the same may be said of his value to Nottinghamshire whom he joined in 1978. In 1981 his 105 wickets at under 15 each and his 745 runs helped them to win their first championship for 52 years.

FIRST-CLASS CAREER (1971/2-)

Inns	NO	HS	Runs	Avge	100s
276	45	142*	6234	26.98	7

Wkts	Avge	Best	5 Wkts	Ct
815	19.76	7-23	47	103

TEST MATCHES (44)

Inns	NO	HS	Runs	Avge	100s
77	11	103	1601	24.25	1

Wkts	Avge	Best	5 Wkts	Ct
200	25.82	7-23	15	22

GREAT CRICKETERS

WALTER REGINALD HAMMOND
(1903-1965)

Walter Hammond's name appears automatically on any list of great English batsmen. His career fell almost entirely between the two World Wars and began, somewhat unusually for a great player, with his earning a reputation as a bold, if polished hitter. He was more than that. He soon became a batsman of impressive command, superbly balanced, quick and powerful, with a classical off-drive.

In 1928-29, when he was still only 25, he turned on the Australians who had been spared a first meeting with him in 1926 by his illness. In the series he made 905 runs, a number still only exceeded by Bradman's 974 in 1930. His 336 not out against New Zealand at Auckland in 1933 remained the highest in Test cricket until Hutton's 364 in 1938. He was a majestic sight when in full flow for Gloucestershire and England in the 10 years before the Second World War.

In 1938 he turned amateur and was appointed captain of England in that summer's series against Australia. He made 240 in the Lord's Test and when he led England in South Africa that winter he added three more 100s including 140 in the last innings of the famous Timeless Test when England made 654 for five in Durban.

After service in the RAF he returned to Gloucestershire and averaged 84.90 in 1946 heading the first-class averages. He resumed the England captaincy and took the team to Australia in 1946-47. But he was 43 and at the top level he could not recover his best form. Nor, as a rather silent and unbending figure, was he a gifted leader of younger men. He soon retired but left many memories not only of his glorious batting but of lively fast-medium bowling and brilliant slip catching. His 78 catches in 1928 remains the most ever held in a season.

FIRST-CLASS CAREER (1920-51)

Inns	NO	HS	Runs	Avge	100s
1005	104	336*	50551	56.10	167

Wkts	Avge	Best	5 Wkts	Ct	St
732	30.58	9-23	22	819	3

TEST MATCHES (85)

Inns	NO	HS	Runs	Avge	100s
140	16	336*	7249	58.45	22

Wkts	Avge	Best	5 Wkts	Ct
83	37.80	5-36	2	110

HANIF MOHAMMAD

(1934-)

Hanif Mohammad, eldest of five brothers who played for Pakistan or came near to it, holds two records which have only a remote chance of being beaten. He has played the highest innings in first-class cricket, 499, and the longest, 16 hours 10 minutes, this when he made 337 not out for Pakistan against West Indies in Barbados in 1957-58.

If this suggests unusual qualities of application and patience, it is an accurate reflection, though occasionally he would produce a flow of fine strokes which were a reminder that he was a batsman of the highest class.

Only five feet six inches in height and little over nine stone in weight, he was an ideal anchor for a Pakistan innings in the years when his country was new to Test cricket. In 1954, when only 19, he defied the strong England bowling of the day at Lord's for three and a half hours to earn a draw. In later years he was much affected by a knee injury which would often take him off the field but he was still a well-enough equipped batsman to make 187 not out in nine hours at Lord's in 1967. By then he was the Pakistan captain but he was too quiet and withdrawn to be an ideal leader.

FIRST-CLASS CAREER (1951/2-1975/6)

Inns	NO	HS	Runs	Avge	100s
370	44	499	17059	52.32	55

Wkts	Avge	Best	5 Wkts	Ct	St
53	28.58	3-4	–	·177	12

TEST MATCHES (55)

Inns	NO	HS	Runs	Avge	100s
97	8	337	3915	43.98	12

Wkts	Avge	Best	5 Wkts	Ct	St
1	95.00	1-1	–	40	–

GEORGE HERBERT HIRST

(1871-1954)

George Hirst's position as one of the greatest all-rounders in cricket history is secure. No other all-rounder is ever likely to score 2000 runs and take 200 wickets in the same season as he did in 1906. His 341 against Leicestershire at Leicester in 1905 remains the highest ever made for Yorkshire, a county of many great batsmen, and at Bath in 1906 he made a hundred in each innings beside taking 11 Somerset wickets in the match.

Hirst began as a left-arm fast-medium bowler and he had already played in Test matches in Australia and England, with more success as a batsman than a bowler, when he acquired a devastating late swing into the bat which gave his bowling a new menace. In 1902 he and his friend and Yorkshire colleague, Wilfred Rhodes, bowled out Australia for 36 at Edgbaston. Later in that series their famous last wicket partnership at the Oval produced the 15 runs needed for victory.

Though his Test career ended in 1909, he was still a good enough player after the War to set Yorkshire cricket off to a flying start again by making 180 not out in the first match against MCC. He retired soon afterwards and became coach at Eton where he produced many successful sides and fine players.

FIRST-CLASS CAREER (1891-1929)

Inns	NO	HS	Runs	Avge	100s
1217	152	341	36356	34.13	60

Wkts	Avge	Best	5 Wkts	Ct
2733	18.74	9-23	184	549

TEST MATCHES (24)

Inns	NO	HS	Runs	Avge	100s
38	3	85	790	22.57	-

Wkts	Avge	Best	5 Wkts	Ct
59	30.00	5-48	3	18

GREAT CRICKETERS

SIR JOHN BERRY HOBBS
(1882-1963)

Jack Hobbs was the greatest batsman of his generation; a complete batsman, classical in method, calm in temperament and supremely efficient in execution. Roughly from the retirement of WG Grace to the heyday of Don Bradman he was without doubt the world's most accomplished batsman. He made more first-class 100s than any other player before or since—197—and it is a tribute to his technique that he made 98 of them after he reached 40.

Born in Cambridge, Hobbs qualified for Surrey in 1905 when he was already 22. He played for Surrey until 1934 and it was only four years before his retirement that he ceased to play for England. Many of his records still stand including the 316 not out against Middlesex, still the highest innings ever played at Lord's. He made an ideal partner at the wicket and formed long and successful opening partnerships with Tom Hayward and Andrew Sandham for Surrey and with the Yorkshireman, Herbert Sutcliffe, for England. With another Yorkshireman, Wilfred Rhodes, he made 323 in Melbourne in 1911-12, still the highest opening stand for England against Australia.

Hobbs' method was simple, graceful and correct, based on a fine eye, a supreme judgment of length, timing and the ability always to be in the right position. He would not bludgeon the bowler but would dictate to him with a steady flow of scoring strokes. The skill which made him a superb player on bad pitches did not desert him even after the age of 50. In 1934 he answered a personal request to play in George Duckworth's benefit match by going to Old Trafford, putting on 184 with Sandham and scoring 116 and 51 not out against Lancashire, that year's champions.

FIRST-CLASS CAREER (1905-34)

Inns	NO	HS	Runs	Avge	100s
1315	106	316*	61237	50.65	197

Wkts	Avge	Best	5 Wkts	Ct
108	24.89	7-56	3	332

TEST MATCHES (61)

Inns	NO	HS	Runs	Avge	100s
102	7	211	5410	56.94	15

Wkts	Avge	Best	5 Wkts	Ct
1	165.00	1-19	–	17

GREAT CRICKETERS

SIR LEONARD HUTTON
(1916-)

Len Hutton was just 22 when he made his 364 against Australia at The Oval in 1938, only four years after he had played his first match for Yorkshire. Even without this innings the quality of his batting would have guaranteed him a place among the great English batsmen of all time. Yet probably his most remarkable feat was being able to play at all after the War, for an accident in an Army gymnasium had left him with his left arm shorter and weaker than his right.

It was as a technician that he was preeminent, a marvellously correct batsman, stylish if not spectacular, always in the right position. He had boundless patience but when he unloosed his superb strokes, it was a sight to remember and his 37 in 24 minutes one morning in a Sydney Test is often recalled as a great innings in cameo form.

As early as 1937 he was making ten hundreds in a season and by 1949 he had conquered his disability to such an extent that he made over 3000 runs. In Australia in 1950-51 he played Lindwall and Miller at their fastest so well that he averaged 88.83, 50 more than the next batsman.

In 1952 Hutton became the first professional in modern times to captain England which he did with much success for three years, regaining the Ashes in 1953 and holding them in Australia 3-1 two winters later. A profound thinker on the game, he seemed to find captaincy on the field no great strain but by 1955 the overall burden of the job had taken more than had been realised out of a quiet reserved man not blessed with the most robust physique. Though only 39 and by no means in decline as a batsman, he had to drop out of Test cricket and, after an interrupted season for Yorkshire, out of first-class cricket.

FIRST-CLASS CAREER (1934-60)

Inns	NO	HS	Runs	Avge	100s
814	91	364	40140	55.51	129

Wkts	Avge	Best	5 Wkts	Ct
173	29.42	6-76	4	399

TEST MATCHES (79)

Inns	NO	HS	Runs	Avge	100s
138	15	364	6971	56.67	19

Wkts	Avge	Best	5 Wkts	Ct
3	77.33	1-2	-	57

GREAT CRICKETERS

JAMES CHARLES LAKER
(1922-   )

If there is any cricket record which is never likely to be broken, it is Jim Laker's 19 wickets for 90 runs for England against Australia at Old Trafford in 1956. No one else has taken more than 17 in a match. Laker's feat was spread over four days of a rain-interrupted match but though the pitch took spin from an early stage, it was not as lethal as many at that period and another highly skilled spinner, Tony Lock, took only one.

A tall strong off-spinner, Jim Laker had a good lively high action, great powers of spin and immaculate control of length, spin and flight. On uncovered pitches in England he mostly pushed the ball through at a pace which stopped the batsmen from moving out to him. On harder pitches overseas, where he had a good but inevitably less spectacular record, he could flight it with equal control.

A Yorkshireman stationed in London at the end of the War, he joined Surrey in 1946 and played a big part in their seven-year runs of championship victories from 1952. He was still learning his craft in 1948 and did not greatly exercise Bradman's Australians that year. But in 1950 on a drying pitch at Bradford he took eight for 2 in a Test trial and it became clear that he was now a spin bowler who would make the very utmost of favourable conditions. In 1953 he and Lock bowled out Australia in the second innings of the final Test at The Oval to enable England to recover the Ashes and, though he was not chosen for the 1954-55 tour of Australia, he began his great year of 1956 by taking all 10 Australian wickets when Surrey became the first county for 44 years to beat an Australian side. After leaving Surrey in 1959 he played some seasons with Essex in the 1960s before becoming a successful television commentator.

FIRST-CLASS CAREER (1946-1964/5)

Inns	NO	HS	Runs	Avge	100s
548	108	113	7304	16.60	2

Wkts	Avge	Best	5 Wkts	Ct
1944	18.41	10-53	127	270

TEST MATCHES (46)

Inns	NO	HS	Runs	Avge	100s
63	15	63	676	14.08	-

Wkts	Avge	Best	5 Wkts	Ct
193	21.24	10-53	9	12

GREAT CRICKETERS

HAROLD LARWOOD
(1904-)

Most of his contemporaries considered Harold Larwood to be the fastest and best fast bowler in cricket history. All the sadder, therefore, that his career should have declined after 1932-33 amid the bitterness of the 'Bodyline' controversy in which he was a central figure.

Fair-haired, of medium height and build, he ran up only about 18 yards but with perfect rhythm and acceleration. Within two years of starting with Nottinghamshire as a 20-year-old ex-miner he was playing for England. His supple, easy, textbook action left no doubt that, given full fitness and fast pitches, he would not be played easily by any batsman. From his action he derived exceptional control and it was this as well as his great pace which made him so deadly when in Australia in 1932-33 Douglas Jardine developed the plan to undo Bradman and other Australian batsmen by bowling at their bodies.

Larwood's success in implementing this policy brought him 33 wickets at under 20 each but from constantly banging his left foot down he suffered an injury from which he never really recovered, though he played for Nottinghamshire until 1938. This and the efforts to repair the damage done to Anglo-Australian relations by the tour caused the second half of his career to be an anti-climax. He was never as fast again and bowled off a short run but he remained no mean batsman at number nine, hitting the ball hard from a sound technique.

After the Second World War he emigrated to Australia with his family. A quiet diffident man, he was welcomed there and lived happily in Sydney, much liked by all. In 1983 he was made an honorary member of the Sydney Cricket Ground.

FIRST-CLASS CAREER (1924-38)

Inns	NO	HS	Runs	Avge	100s
438	72	102*	7290	19.91	3

Wkts	Avge	Best	5 Wkts	Ct
1427	17.51	9-41	97	236

TEST MATCHES (21)

Inns	NO	HS	Runs	Avge	100s
28	3	98	485	19.40	-

Wkts	Avge	Best	5 Wkts	Ct
78	28.35	6-32	4	15

GREAT CRICKETERS

DENNIS KEITH LILLEE
(1949-   )

Dennis Lillee's main achievement was not that he became the best fast bowler of his day in the 1970s but that in doing so he showed that even fast bowlers can overcome injuries which would once have ended a career in sport. He was already on the threshold of a great career and had taken 31 wickets in a Test series in England when he suffered stress fractures of the lower spine.

No one believed then that he would again be a genuinely fast bowler of the highest class but by hard work and determination Lillee fought his way back to destroy England, with Jeff Thomson, in the 1974-75 series. Fully restored, largely by his dedication to keeping fit, he kept on taking wickets, moving the ball with his fine action with such control that as he passed 30 he could achieve by subtlety and varying of pace what once he had achieved by being very, very fast.

Those who found unattractive his avowed intention of often bowling at the batsman's body, his disregard for convention and his stirring-up of an excitable crowd, did not stint their admiration for him as a bowler when not trying to intimidate the batsman. Apart from odd periods, such as on the dead pitches of Pakistan, he remained consistently successful. Before he became one of the leading lights of the Packer World Series Cricket he took 11 wickets in Australia's narrow win over England in the historic Centenary Test in Melbourne. Four years later in England he was still a good enough bowler to take 39 wickets in a series in England.

FIRST-CLASS CAREER (1969/70-   )

Inns	NO	HS	Runs	Avge	100s
210	61	73*	2134	14.32	-

Wkts	Avge	Best	5 Wkts	Ct
786	22.65	8-29	46	57

TEST MATCHES (65)

Inns	NO	HS	Runs	Avge	100s
86	22	73*	874	13.65	-

Wkts	Avge	Best	5 Wkts	Ct
335	23.46	7-83	22	21

Editor's note: Lillee announced his retirement at the end of the 1983-84 Test series with Pakistan, having taken 355 Test wickets (average 23.92).

GREAT CRICKETERS

RAYMOND RUSSELL LINDWALL
(1921-   )

Ray Lindwall swiftly made his name as the greatest fast bowler in the world when international cricket was resumed after the Second World War. His arm was slightly lower than the coaching manuals advise but in every other feature his accelerating run-up and balanced controlled action were a model which helped to extend his career until his middle 30s by which time his pace was a lesser weapon than his accuracy and considerable movement of the ball. Of only slightly above medium height, he was in interesting contrast with his partner of many years, the tall dynamic Keith Miller.

Together they plagued many opponents, first for New South Wales, until Lindwall moved to Queensland for six seasons from 1954-55, but most memorably for Australia against opponents who were well equipped in high-class batting. The bowling of both England and West Indies may have been thin then but those were the days in England of Hutton, Compton, Washbrook, WJ Edrich, Simpson and even, in 1946-47 an ageing Hammond. For West Indies it was the era of the three Ws, Weekes, Worrell and Walcott, Stollmeyer and Rae.

Unlike his successor, Dennis Lillee, two decades later, Ray Lindwall used the fast short ball only to provide occasional variety and he left behind him a reputation among cricketers of being a fair fast bowler in the classical mould.

FIRST-CLASS CAREER (1941/2-1961/2)

Inns	NO	HS	Runs	Avge	100s
270	39	134*	5042	21.82	5

Wkts	Avge	Best	5 Wkts	Ct
794	21.35	7-20	34	123

TEST MATCHES (61)

Inns	NO	HS	Runs	Avge	100s
84	13	118	1502	21.15	2

Wkts	Avge	Best	5 Wkts	Ct
228	23.03	7-38	12	26

CLIVE HUBERT LLOYD

(1944-   )

Clive Lloyd's long career and his long tenure of the captaincy of West Indies are a tribute to a remarkable but highly effective method as a batsman and a temperament which saved many a batting collapse and in other ways earned respect from his contemporaries. He was lucky to have strong West Indian bowling sides under him and batsmen of the capacity of Vivian Richards and Gordon Greenidge. But without being regarded as a brilliant captain he became a highly regarded one with a record of success few could touch.

As a gangling bespectacled left-handed giant, he did not look a world-class batsman at first sight. He was exciting to watch but the casual watcher would have said that he relied too much on sheer power to be consistently successful on all pitches. Yet that powerful frame did not stop him, in his youth, from being a cover-point of panther-like agility; and behind that power and the swinging of the bat in huge arcs was a basic straightness.

Allied to the fact that his mishits would still go for four and in unusual directions, this made him both a fast scorer and a batsman difficult to shift. Just as his great reach would allow him to drive a ball which was of a good length to a normal batsman, so it served him equally well when he was called on to defend. He has been, in fact, amazingly consistent, an unusual type of anchor of many West Indian sides and of Lancashire from 1968, latterly as captain.

FIRST-CLASS CAREER (1963/4-   )

Inns	NO	HS	Runs	Avge	100s
674	87	242*	28660	48.82	74

Wkts	Avge	Best	5 Wkts	Ct
114	36.00	4-48	-	345

TEST MATCHES (90)

Inns	NO	HS	Runs	Avge	100s
149	10	242*	6238	44.87	16

Wkts	Avge	Best	5 Wkts	Ct
10	62.20	2-13	-	68

GREAT CRICKETERS

PETER BARKER HOWARD MAY
(1929-)

For a time in the 1960s Peter May was almost certainly the best batsman on all pitches in the world and many well placed to judge consider him the best batsman England has produced since the War. His Test career spanned barely ten years, yet apart from being the mainstay of the batting for most of that period, he also captained England a record 41 times.

His record, fine as it is, conceals two facts. One is that during his career for Surrey, whom he also captained for four years, twice as champions, he was batting on pitches at The Oval, and elsewhere, which were less true than today's and on which the great Surrey bowlers of the day, Bedser and Loader, Laker and Lock, were taking hundreds of wickets. He also suffered the handicap of seldom going to the crease for England without feeling that if he failed, the side failed, for in his era England were wont to surrender depth of batting to strength of bowling, having many fine bowlers available.

May played very straight and had all the strokes except perhaps the hook which he did not often seem to need. Tall, slim and elegant, yet broad shouldered and powerful, he combined the classic style of the old-fashioned amateur with the modern professional competitiveness. His stature can be gauged from the fact that in the low-scoring series of 1956 against Australia he averaged 90, double that of the next batsman who played throughout the series.

After a period of ill health he retired in 1961 aged 31. He had played as an amateur and he continued to serve the game on countless committees for Surrey and MCC, as chairman of the TCCB cricket committee, as President of MCC in 1981 and from 1982 as chairman of selectors.

FIRST-CLASS CAREER (1948-63)

Inns	NO	HS	Runs	Avge	100s
618	77	285*	27592	51.00	85

Wkts	Avge	Best	5 Wkts	Ct
-	-	-	-	282

TEST MATCHES (66)

Inns	NO	HS	Runs	Avge	100s
106	9	285*	4537	46.77	13

Wkts	Avge	Best	5 Wkts	Ct
-	-	-	-	42

GREAT CRICKETERS

WILFRED RHODES
(1877-1973)

Few players have had as long and versatile a career as Wilfred Rhodes who first played for Yorkshire in 1898 as a left-arm spin bowler with a classic action and took 154 wickets in his first season. Next year he played in his first Test match and in the next he took 261 wickets.

For five years, in which he took 1251 wickets, he batted low in the order for Yorkshire but his defence was sound, he was not short of strokes and by 1909-10 he was opening the England innings in Johannesburg with Hobbs. They made 159 together then, 221 later in the series and in Melbourne two years later the 323 which is still the highest opening stand for England against Australia.

By that time he was not bowling much for England—only 18 overs in the 1911-12 series and only 25 in the Triangular Tournament of 1912 in England. Yet after the War he returned to Yorkshire aged 42 with his bowling restored to such an extent that he took 325 wickets in the first two seasons and was still taking 100 wickets in a season when 51.

Though he resumed after the War by opening the England innings with Hobbs, he did little with bat or ball and dropped out of Test cricket until, in one of the game's most famous come-backs, he was recalled aged 48 for the final Test at The Oval in 1926. In the two innings he made 44 runs at number seven and in 45 overs took six for 79, a major contribution to England's recovery of the Ashes. He was not quite finished yet, for he went on the 1929-30 tour of West Indies and remains the oldest Test player at 52 years 165 days.

FIRST-CLASS CAREER (1898-1930)

Inns	NO	HS	Runs	Avge	100s
1534	237	267*	39969	30.81	58

Wkts	Avge	Best	5 Wkts	Ct
4187	16.70	9-24	286	756

TEST MATCHES (58)

Inns	NO	HS	Runs	Avge	100s
98	21	179	2325	30.19	2

Wkts	Avge	Best	5 Wkts	Ct
127	26.96	8-68	6	60

GREAT CRICKETERS

BARRY ANDERSON RICHARDS
(1945-   )

Barry Richards was almost certainly the most gifted batsman of his day and in his late 20s, the early 1970s, played many innings which few batsmen of any era could have surpassed. No one present will forget his first Test hundred for South Africa against Australia in 1970, almost 100 before lunch on the first day, as near the perfect innings in range and execution as one could ask to see. His second hundred in Port Elizabeth showed him in a different mood. He often fretted if tied down, even for just an over or two, and this time he reacted by hitting his second 50 with a violence which was out of character with the easy elegance of his normal graceful strokeplay. Another innings remembered for ever by those who watched it was played during a season with South Australia when he made 325 not out in a five and a half hour day against the young Lillee and other Western Australian bowlers in Perth.

Ever disappointed at not being able to show his talents at Test level after 1970, he frequently gave the sad impression that, for all his brilliant talents, he did not enjoy his cricket, anyhow as he knew it during his highly successful 10½ seasons with Hampshire. He often played as if he was bored with hitting the ball for four or six with strokes which thrilled his audience. Tall, fair, with lightning reflexes, in the slips as well as at the crease. He was a batsman almost impossible for any critic to fault technically, a great batsman robbed, alas, by politics of showing just how great.

FIRST-CLASS CAREER (1964/5-1982/3)

Inns	NO	HS	Runs	Avge	100s
576	58	356	28358	54.74	80

Wkts	Avge	Best	5 Wkts	Ct
77	37.48	7-63	1	367

TEST MATCHES (4)

Inns	NO	HS	Runs	Avge	100s
7	-	140	508	72.57	2

Wkts	Avge	Best	5 Wkts	Ct
1	26.00	1-12	-	3

ISAAC VIVIAN ALEXANDER RICHARDS
(1952-   )

From Antigua in the Leeward Islands Vivian Richards made his way via Somerset into the West Indies Test team, scored 192 not out in his second Test match in India in 1974-75 and has seldom hesitated since. He became probably the world's best batsman of the day and certainly the most consistently destructive. His confidence and at times utter command of the bowling leads him to attempt strokes which are not always prudent and sometimes he pays for them. But with his instant reflexes and quick-footedness he can score runs at a rate which no one without his inventiveness could approach in the conditions.

Sometimes his batting has an almost casual air about it, as if it is too easy to be taken seriously. But on the big occasions, especially in the limited-over finals at Lord's, he has usually been in his element—138 not out in the Prudential final of 1979, 117 in the same year's Gillette final, 132 not out in the 1981 Benson and Hedges final; and in between them 145 in the Lord's Test match of 1980. His improvisation reached new heights near the end of his Prudential innings when, being offered an inslanting ball near his toes which would have severely restricted most mortals, he somehow pivoted and with bat vertical hit it for six behind square-leg.

As a fielder, he can be transformed in a flash from slouching inactivity into an acrobat with a deadly throw. As a bowler of off-spin or gentle medium pace he can maintain an accuracy which has often led impatient batsmen to their downfall.

FIRST-CLASS CAREER (1971/2-   )

Inns	NO	HS	Runs	Avge	100s
490	35	291	22630	49.73	69

Wkts	Avge	Best	5 Wkts	Ct	St
136	42.11	5-88	1	282	1

TEST MATCHES (52)

Inns	NO	HS	Runs	Avge	100s
80	4	291	4411	58.03	14

Wkts	Avge	Best	5 Wkts	Ct	St
14	56.42	2-19	-	56	-

SIR GARFIELD ST AUBRUN SOBERS
(1936-)

Gary Sobers sets himself apart from the world's other great all-rounders in cricket history because he not only batted, bowled and fielded brilliantly but bowled at Test level in three different styles, as a left-arm fast-medium bowler, an orthodox left-arm spinner and as an exponent of chinaman and googly highly effective as a variation in a side usually well stocked with fast bowling.

It was as an orthodox left-arm spinner and useful batsman from Barbados that he first played for West Indies against England in 1954 aged 17. Four years later he made his Test record 365 not out against Pakistan, somewhat uncharacteristically for it took him over 10 hours. Most of his later innings were played, when responsibility to the side allowed, with a dashing freedom of stroke and usually some classical samples of the left-hander's off-drive.

He was already just about the best all-rounder in the world when during three seasons with South Australia he turned himself into a superb fast-medium bowler with a lissom action and the ability to move the ball a lot. Inevitably he succeeded Frank Worrell as captain and it was typical of his cavalier approach even to Test cricket that in 1967-68 against England he should make a rare piece of Test history by declaring and losing.

In 1968, with the instant registration of overseas players, he joined Nottinghamshire for seven seasons but though he lifted them at once from 16th to fourth, a persistent knee injury, added to the burden of playing in all seasons, wore him down. Soon after making 150 not out in West Indies' rout of England at Lord's in 1973, he dropped out of cricket at the top level.

FIRST-CLASS CAREER (1952/3-1974)

Inns	NO	HS	Runs	Avge	100s
609	93	365*	28315	54.87	86

Wkts	Avge	Best	5 Wkts	Ct
1043	27.74	9-49	36	407

TEST MATCHES (93)

Inns	NO	HS	Runs	Avge	100s
160	21	365*	8032	57.78	26

Wkts	Avge	Best	5 Wkts	Ct
235	34.03	6-73	6	109

HERBERT SUTCLIFFE

(1894-1978)

To casual readers of cricket history Herbert Sutcliffe might seem to have been the junior member of two famous opening partnerships—Hobbs and Sutcliffe for England, Holmes and Sutcliffe for Yorkshire. His record, however, especially in Test matches, earned him a place among the most successful batsmen in English cricket history. There are few batting feats more remarkable than his in the wet summer of 1931 when he averaged 96.96. Nobody else averaged over 70. His Test average of 60.73, in 84 innings, is the highest of any Englishman, higher than his overall career average of 52.

Compared with most batsmen of similar achievement, he had fewer natural gifts. He was essentially a player who made the most of his ability, without glitter but with an abundance of practical good sense and with complete composure. His smooth dark hair and well groomed appearance never seemed ruffled and he excelled on the big occasion. His judgment was impeccable and if he was not a genius, he had a record which many a genius would envy.

His most famous, and perhaps most valuable, stand with Hobbs was that of 172 on a wet pitch at The Oval in 1926. A brilliant piece of batting it ensured the recovery of the Ashes. With Percy Holmes his best remembered stand is the 555 against Essex at Leyton in 1932 which was to stand as a world record for 44 years. Sutcliffe's contribution was 313.

FIRST-CLASS CAREER (1919-45)

Inns	NO	HS	Runs	Avge	100s
1088	123	313	50138	51.95	149

Wkts	Avge	Best	5 Wkts	Ct
10	49.20	2-16	-	466

TEST MATCHES (54)

Inns	NO	HS	Runs	Avge	100s
84	9	194	4555	60.73	16

Wkts	Avge	Best	5 Wkts	Ct
-	-	-	-	23

GREAT CRICKETERS

FREDERICK SEWARDS TRUEMAN
(1931-   )

'Characters' in cricket are more generally appreciated as they grow older and, though Fred Trueman's ability as a fast bowler was fully appreciated from his first appearance for Yorkshire aged 18, his career was from time to time attended by controversy. It would have needed a crystal ball to foresee that he would finish up on the Yorkshire committee and as an advocate of stern discipline, as did happen.

Squarely built and of medium height, he had a curving run-up with good acceleration and an action which needed only a little adjustment in his early years to produce accuracy as well as pace. After doing national service he had immediate success in his first Test series in 1952 when he was much too fast on lively pitches for the Indians. His first tour, in West Indies in 1953-54, was not considered a success on or off the field and as by then young bowlers of the calibre of Statham, Tyson and Loader were available as well as Bedser and Trevor Bailey, he was not included in the England party which held the Ashes in Australia in 1954-55.

With time, however, he matured into a bowler of the highest class who had great pace but did most of his damage through the amount he could swing the ball and move it off the pitch. He remained a fine bowler into his 30s and after many successes approached 300 Test wickets. He was already easily the biggest wicket-taker in Test history and there was great rejoicing at The Oval against Australia in 1964 when he took the 300th. He dropped out of Test cricket next year and played his last match for Yorkshire in 1968.

FIRST-CLASS CAREER (1949-69)

Inns	NO	HS	Runs	Avge	100s
713	120	104	9231	15.56	3

Wkts	Avge	Best	5 Wkts	Ct
2304	18.29	8-28	126	438

TEST MATCHES (67)

Inns	NO	HS	Runs	Avge	100s
85	14	39*	981	13.81	-

Wkts	Avge	Best	5 Wkts	Ct
307	21.57	8-31	17	64

VICTOR THOMAS TRUMPER
(1877-1915)

Victor Trumper died during World War I when not yet 40 but he left a name for grace and elegance which gave him a special place among the great batsmen of cricket history. He first played for New South Wales when only 17 but it was another four years before he really announced himself with a maiden hundred which he extended to 292 not out. Within another three years, the charm and classical skill of his batting had captured a huge public, especially in England in 1899 and 1902.

Wonderfully quick on his feet, he was a masterly judge of length, always well balanced, so it seemed, always ready with the right stroke. Unlike many Australian batsmen, he was not seriously inconvenienced by bad pitches and in the unusually wet English summer of 1902 he made 2570 runs.

For most of his Test career he opened the innings and in 1902 launched a famous Test at Old Trafford with an innings of 104 before lunch on the first day. His third and fourth visits to England in 1905 and 1909 were much less successful but at home in 1910-11 he was largely responsible for destroying the great South African googly bowlers of the day. He averaged 94 and his 214 not out at Adelaide took only four hours.

He scored 113 against England in the first Test of 1911-12 and when he made 293 for an Australian XI in New Zealand, he shared with Arthur Sims in a stand of 433 which is still a world record for the eighth wicket. It lasted only just over three hours but it was Trumper's last great innings. Within 16 months he had died of Bright's Disease.

FIRST-CLASS CAREER (1894/5-1913/4)

Inns	NO	HS	Runs	Avge	100s
401	21	300*	16939	44.57	42

Wkts	Avge	Best	5 Wkts	Ct
64	31.73	5-19	2	171

TEST MATCHES (48)

Inns	NO	HS	Runs	Avge	100s
89	8	214*	3163	39.04	8

Wkts	Avge	Best	5 Wkts	Ct
8	39.62	3-60	-	31

CLYDE LEOPOLD WALCOTT
(1926-   )

The largest and most powerful of the 'Three Ws' who dominated West Indian cricket during and after the Second World War, Clyde Walcott wrote his name in the record books just as often as Everton Weekes and Sir Frank Worrell. Strictly in terms of class he was perhaps a shade below them, lacking the compact soundness and lightning feet of Weekes and the elegance of Worrell. But he was a tremendous driver and hooker who reached his peak in 1954-55 against Australia in the Caribbean. His 827 runs in that series have been exceeded only four times and his five separate hundreds are the most ever made in a series.

He was only 16 when he first played for Barbados during the War and only 20 when in 1946 he and the year-older Worrell put on 574 in an unbroken stand for the fourth wicket against Trinidad. In his first Test early in 1948 Walcott opened the innings but he achieved little in the series and kept his place as an efficient but somewhat unlikely looking 6ft 2in wicketkeeper.

He kept wicket again on the triumphant tour of England in 1950 but this time made a lot of runs including 168 not out in the Lord's Test, the first won by West Indies in England. He played Lindwall and Miller indifferently in Australia in 1951-52, averaging only 14 in his three Tests, but when England under Leonard Hutton arrived in West Indies in 1954, his average shot up to 87 and he was embarked on his most prolific period, which lasted until England's next visit in 1960. His Test career ended during that tour but he continued to captain British Guiana for some years and served West Indian cricket in various capacities thereafter, notably as manager of touring teams.

FIRST-CLASS CAREER (1941/2-1963/4)

Inns	NO	HS	Runs	Avge	100s
238	29	314*	11820	56.55	40

Wkts	Avge	Best	5 Wkts	Ct	St
35	36.25	5-41	1	175	33

TEST MATCHES (44)

Inns	NO	HS	Runs	Avge	100s
74	7	220	3798	56.68	15

Wkts	Avge	Best	5 Wkts	Ct	St
11	37.09	3-50	-	53	11

GREAT CRICKETERS

EVERTON DE COURCY WEEKES
(1925-   )

Everton Weekes, smaller in stature than the other two of the 'Three Ws', was the most brilliant on his day—and his day was a frequent occurrence. In 1955-56 in New Zealand he made five successive hundreds, a feat only three batsmen have beaten. No one has equalled his five successive Test hundreds, one against England in 1947-48, four in India a year later.

Wonderfully quick into position, Weekes at times recalled Don Bradman in his range of ruthless strokes played off front foot and back with flawless judgement and impeccable timing. He first played for Barbados in 1944 but until he made his 141 against England in Jamaica in 1948 his entry into Test cricket was disappointing for one of his record.

It was said that without that 141 he might not have been chosen for the Indian tour. But he went—and averaged 90 in all matches, so that he arrived in England in 1950 with a reputation for prolific scoring which he promptly embellished. In the first half of the tour he made scores of over 200 five times and it was not until he scored 129 in a classical stand of 283 with Frank Worrell in the Trent Bridge Test in July that he failed to turn 100 into 200.

Except in Australia in 1951-52 his success continued, at all levels of cricket including the League, until the middle 1950s when he became increasingly dogged by sinus trouble and injuries. It was not until the last match of the 1957 tour of England that he made his only 100 of the summer but he played an innings of 90 with a broken finger in the Lord's Test which is still remembered as a gem of strokeplay. He made runs against Pakistan that winter but not with the old facility and retired from Test cricket to become a successful captain/coach of Barbados and later an international bridge player.

FIRST-CLASS CAREER (1944/5-1964)

Inns	NO	HS	Runs	Avge	100s
241	24	304*	12010	55.34	36

Wkts	Avge	Best	5 Wkts	Ct	St
17	43.00	4-38	-	125	1

TEST MATCHES (48)

Inns	NO	HS	Runs	Avge	100s
81	5	207	4455	58.61	15

Wkts	Avge	Best	5 Wkts	Ct
1	77.00	1-8	-	49

FRANK EDWARD WOOLLEY

(1887-1978)

Frank Woolley was one of those cricketers who earn a special place in the game's history for an unusual career and his method of batting. He played for Kent from 1906 to 1938. He played for England in 1909 and on numerous occasions afterwards until 1934 when, aged 47, he was brought back not only as a batsman but as a wicket-keeper. In his younger day he was a good enough left-arm slow bowler to take 100 wickets in a season eight times. Though his Test record was not outstanding, his aggregate of first-class runs, 58,959, is second only to that of Jack Hobbs.

Yet this varied record is not the reason for his unique place in the memories of those who saw him. What was different was the way in which he made his runs. Very tall, with a dignified unhurried manner, he was a majestic figure. There was majesty, too, in the full swing of the bat which, with his superb timing, allowed him to drive effortlessly—and, because of his great reach, more often than most batsmen. Whether batting or bowling he did nothing ungraceful, nothing crude or violent, yet he was without rivals as a controlled hitter of the ball. His method is often said to have been influenced by playing for Kent in his youth with several talented amateurs of the day.

By contrast with Colin Cowdrey, a Kent hero of later years who made 22 of his 107 hundreds in Test matches, Woolley made only five Test hundreds in 145. It is typical of his career that he is remembered more for smaller innings such as his 95 and 93 in a losing cause against the formidable Australians of 1921 at Lord's and a delightful 41 at the start of the famous 1930 Test there.

FIRST-CLASS CAREER (1906-38)

Inns	NO	HS	Runs	Avge	100s
1530	84	305*	58959	40.77	145

Wkts	Avge	Best	5 Wkts	Ct
2068	19.85	8-22	117	1018

TEST MATCHES (64)

Inns	NO	HS	Runs	Avge	100s
98	7	154	3283	36.07	5

Wkts	Avge	Best	5 Wkts	Ct
83	33.91	7-76	4	64

SIR FRANK MORTIMER WORRELL
(1924-1967)

Frank Worrell's career began, like those of Walcott and Weekes, in war-time cricket in Barbados but differed slightly after his first Test series in that he went to play League cricket in England which led to his taking a degree at Manchester University. His career lasted longer than those of the other two, for though less of a force with bat and ball, he was still a highly successful captain of West Indies in 1963. Knighted in 1964, he had started another career at the University of the West Indies when he died from leukaemia aged 42.

Worrell had first played for Barbados as a left-arm spinner but as he became known as one of the world's great batsmen, orthodox, cultured and with more patience when it was needed than many West Indians, he also became a top class left-arm fast-medium bowler and thus one of the great all-rounders of the day.

In 1950 his innings of 261 in the Trent Bridge Test was acclaimed as a classic. In a less successful side in 1957 he saved West Indies on the same ground by playing right through the innings, making 191 not out. Against England in Barbados in 1959-60 he gave a further example of his application and determination in adversity by batting 11 hours 20 minutes for 197 not out.

His assumption of the captaincy in 1960 was immediately followed by one of the most famous tours of all time, the one in Australia which began with the tied Test in Brisbane and ended with West Indies losing 2-1 but being cheered by tens of thousands through the streets of Melbourne.

His leadership on and off the field brought West Indian cricket one of its most successful periods and he retired after the tour of England in 1963, held in great respect by all.

FIRST-CLASS CAREER (1941/2-1964)

Inns	NO	HS	Runs	Avge	100s
326	49	308*	15025	54.24	39

Wkts	Avge	Best	5 Wkts	Ct
349	29.00	7-70	13	137

TEST MATCHES (51)

Inns	NO	HS	Runs	Avge	100s
87	9	261	3860	49.48	9

Wkts	Avge	Best	5 Wkts	Ct
69	38.72	7-70	2	43

THE WORLD CUP

The World Cup was devised by the International Cricket Conference in the early 1970s as an international competition of limited-over cricket (60 overs a side) which would provide a source of income not only for the six (now seven) Test-playing countries but for the associate member-countries whose financial opportunities were few. It was not truly a World Cup, for South Africa, one of the strongest cricketing nations in the world, was excluded.

The choice of England as the country to stage the first tournament in 1975 was not a difficult one and until India and Pakistan began, in 1983, to examine the possibility of holding it jointly in their two countries, the advantages of England as the setting were too numerous to be questioned. The main centres of population are relatively close together, so that little travelling is involved. Adelaide to Perth is 1,700 miles. London and Leeds, the two most widely separated English venues, are less than 200 miles apart. The facilities and communications on grounds are good. The large immigrant populations assure a following for Indians, Pakistanis and West Indians. The midsummer evenings are light, allowing a long day's play if necessary, and the English season falls at a time of year when no other countries are playing. Thus the minimum of disruption is caused to cricket elsewhere. Certainly the weather cannot be guaranteed but two days are allowed for the completion of each match and in 1975, 1979 and 1983, the weather overall was kind.

The competitions followed the basic rules of limited-over cricket existing at the time. No individual bowler was allowed to bowl more than one-fifth (in this case 12) of the allotted overs; by 1983 no more than five fielders were allowed outside a 30 yard oval surrounding the pitch, a rule necessitated by the defensiveness of the bowling and field-placing in limited-over cricket; special regulations were made to meet a severe hold-up by rain; and there was a stricter interpretation of what is a 'wide' than exists in first-class cricket. Otherwise the Laws of Cricket applied.

THE FIRST PRUDENTIAL WORLD CUP, 1975

For the inaugural tournament two associate-member countries, Sri Lanka and East Africa, joined the six Test-playing members of ICC, England, Australia, New Zealand, West Indies, India and Pakistan. The contestants were split into two groups, the four in each group playing each other once. The two leaders in each group went through to the semi-finals. In the final, West Indies defeated Australia by 17 runs at Lord's in a match watched by 26,000 people and lasting from 11 o'clock to 8.45 pm. In the semi-finals Australia had beaten England at Leeds and West Indies had beaten New Zealand at The Oval.

England's defeat at Headingley, Leeds, was remarkable for the left arm fast-medium bowling of Gary Gilmour for

Australia. On a humid morning he swung the ball a
prodigious amount and in his 12 overs took six wickets for 14.
He also made 28 not out when Australia, at 39 for six, were
struggling to pass England's modest 93. In the final the West
Indian captain, Clive Lloyd, made 102 and Australia never
quite promised to beat the West Indies' 291 for eight.

The tournament was played for the Prudential Cup—the
Prudential Assurance Company put £100,000 into the
pool—and the takings came to over £200,000.

THE SECOND, 1979

The competition was voted a great success and it was agreed
to have a second Prudential World Cup in England in 1979, this
time after the staging of a new tournament for the ICC Trophy
in which 14 associate members took part: Argentina,
Bangladesh, Bermuda, Canada, Denmark, Fiji, Holland, Hong
Kong, Israel, Malaysia, Papua New Guinea, Singapore, the
United States and West Africa. A 15th member, Gibraltar, had
to withdraw and a team from Wales took their place. The 15
sides were divided into three groups and the two finalists, Sri
Lanka and Canada, qualified to play in the Prudential Cup
which followed.

The weather during the ICC Trophy competition, played in
the Midlands, was appalling but improved during the
Prudential Cup which was again a success. This time West
Indies beat England in the final by 92 runs. In the semi-finals
West Indies had won a high scoring match against Pakistan at
The Oval and England had held off New Zealand by nine
runs. In the final West Indies owed their victory almost
entirely to a partnership between Vivian Richards, who made
a brilliant 138 not out, and Collis King (86). Through them
West Indies repaired a start of 99 for four. Though Joel Garner
later accelerated England's defeat by taking five wickets for
38 runs, England, who had the better batting conditions in the
second half of the day, had largely thrown away their chance
of winning by scoring too slowly during an opening stand of
129 between Brearley and Boycott. When it ended, 158 runs
were still needed off only 22 overs and the later batsmen lost
their wickets in a vain attack.

This second World Cup tournament was again highly
successful. This time the Prudential's contribution was
£250,000, evidence of world inflation as well as the
competition's popularity.

It was agreed then to make the tournament a four-yearly
event and to hold the next, again under Prudential
sponsorship, in England in 1983. Before that could take place,
however, hard negotiating was required.

With the passing years and the growing commercialism of
cricket, the original worthy idea of helping the funds of
associate-members of ICC was rivalled by other financial

aims. The Australian players, coming from a country where there was now big money in cricket, were said to have been dissatisfied with what they had received in previous World Cups. If Australia did not send a team, a competition already lacking South Africa would fall even shorter of justifying the title 'World Cup'.

More difficult to settle was the English dissatisfaction with previous financial arrangements. The Test and County Cricket Board, promoters of first-class cricket in England, wanted compensation for the loss of one Test match and three one-day international matches which would otherwise have been played against New Zealand, the tourists due in 1983, and which would have earned more than the TCCB's share of the World Cup profits.

There was also a feeling among some of the more ambitious associate-member countries that three of them, not just one, should take part, bringing the field up to ten. By then Sri Lanka, admitted to full membership of the ICC in 1981, ranked as a Test-playing country. This idea was rejected because it would have prolonged the competition to such an extent that the English season would have been badly disrupted. It would also probably have provided more one-sided matches than was desirable. In any case the decision had been taken to extend the preliminary rounds by making each side play the other in its group twice. This enabled the matches to be spread around more grounds.

THE 1983 WORLD CUP

In the end agreement was reached and the tournament was, like that of 1975, blessed by superb weather after a dismal spring. The eighth competitor was Zimbabwe, who had won the place by virtue of their success in another ICC Trophy tournament played a year before, again in the Midlands and again in dreadful weather. Zimbabwe proved stronger opposition than had previous associate-member countries, not surprisingly for until the creation of Zimbabwe they had, as Rhodesia, competed at first-class level in the Currie Cup in South Africa.

One of the weaknesses of an international cricket tournament can be its predictability. Nothing had happened in the intervening years to suggest that West Indies would not keep their title in 1983. Pakistan, who had been growing in strength, were seriously weakened by an injury which prevented their captain, Imran Khan, from bowling. This was enough to rule them out as serious contenders. New Zealand had improved enough to win most of the one-day matches they had played against England during the recent Australasian summer but neither they nor Australia looked good enough to unseat West Indies at the top. As for the other contestants, Sri Lanka and Zimbabwe were bound to be outclassed and India had never seemed well enough

THE WORLD CUP

equipped or even to have the confidence in themselves in this form of cricket to win such a tournament in England.

However, the competition began with two major surprises when Zimbabwe beat Australia by 13 runs at Trent Bridge, Nottingham, and India beat the holders, West Indies, by 34 runs at Old Trafford, Manchester. Neither of these results was considered of deep significance and in fact Zimbabwe lost all their other five matches. But India's win, and their subsequent escape at Tunbridge Wells when their captain Kapil Dev made a brilliant 175 not out after they had been 17 for five against Zimbabwe, meant that when they had beaten an out of form Australia they had qualified for the semi-finals.

In their first match at Old Trafford they had found conditions akin to those in India where fast bowlers are blunted and medium pace and slow bowling can be unusually effective, especially against batsmen trying to score quickly. By chance, the semi-final was also played at Old Trafford. England's fast bowlers were as ineffective as West Indies' had been and India, relying on steady medium pace, triumphed by six wickets.

It had still not occurred to many cricket followers that India, in less favourable conditions in the final at Lord's, would overthrow West Indies, who had easily beaten Pakistan in the other semi-final at The Oval. However, the Lord's pitch, no doubt affected by an unexpectedly wet May followed by sunshine, was slower than usual and again the Indians' medium pace bowlers, Sandhu, Madan Lal and Amarnath, were unexpectedly successful. India were always struggling to reach 183 in 54.4 overs but West Indies had even greater difficulty and, before the astonished eyes of a crowd of over 25,000 and amid frenzied Indian excitement, India won by 43 runs. When the Indian players returned home ten days later, a huge crowd greeted them at Bombay airport and cheered them through 20 miles of streets to the Wankhede Stadium. It was a victory whose style and utter unpredictability on all known form had done much to strengthen the concept of a world cup.

India's captain Kapil Dev hits out during his historic innings against Zimbabwe in the 1983 World Cup.

FIRST CLASS CRICKET RECORDS

These records include all first-class matches played between 1815 and the end of the 1983 English season on 13 September.
* not out (unless otherwise stated)
d innings declared
c innings closed

TEAM RECORDS

HIGHEST INNINGS TOTALS

1107	Victoria v NSW	Melbourne	1926-27
1059	Victoria v Tasmania	Melbourne	1922-23
951-7d	Sind v Baluchistan	Karachi	1973-74
918	NSW v S Australia	Sydney	1900-01
912-8d	Holkar v Mysore	Indore	1945-46
910-6d	Railways v Dera Ismail Khan	Lahore	1964-65
903-7d	England v Australia	The Oval	1938
887	Yorkshire v Warwickshire	Birmingham	1896
849	England v West Indies	Kingston	1929-30
843	Australians v Oxford & Cambridge U Past & Present	Portsmouth	1893
839	NSW v Tasmania	Sydney	1898-99
826-4	Maharashtra v Western India States	Poona	1948-49
824	Lahore Greens v Bahawalpur	Lahore	1965-66
821-7d	S Australia v Queensland	Adelaide	1939-40
815	NSW v Victoria	Sydney	1908-09
811	Surrey v Somerset	The Oval	1899
807	NSW v S Australia	Adelaide	1899-00
805	NSW v Victoria	Melbourne	1905-06
803-4d	Kent v Essex	Brentwood	1934
803	Non-Smokers v Smokers	East Melbourne	1886-87
802	NSW v S Australia	Sydney	1920-21
801	Lancs v Somerset	Taunton	1895

HIGHEST SECOND INNINGS TOTALS

770	NSW v S Australia	Adelaide	1920-21
764	Bombay v Holkar	Bombay	1944-45
761-8d	NSW v Queensland	Sydney	1929-30
726-7d	Barbados v Trinidad	Bridgetown	1926-27
724	Victoria v S Australia	Melbourne	1920-21
714-8d	Bombay v Maharashtra	Poona	1948-49
703-9d	Cambridge U v Sussex	Hove	1890

HIGHEST FOURTH INNINGS TOTALS

To Win

507-7	Cambridge U v MCC	Lord's	1896
502-6	Middx v Notts	Nottingham	1925
502-8	Players v Gentlemen	Lord's	1900
500-7	SA Universities v W Province	Stellenbosch	1978-79

To Draw

654-5	England v S Africa	Durban	1938-39
576-8	Trinidad v Barbados	Port-of-Spain	1945-46
529-9	Combined XI v S Africans	Perth	1963-64

To Lose

604	Maharashtra v Bombay	Poona	1948-49
572	NSW v S Australia	Sydney	1907-08
518	Victoria v Queensland	Brisbane	1926-27

HIGHEST MATCH AGGREGATES

Runs-Wkts

2376-37 Bombay v Maharashtra	Poona	1948-49
2078-40 Bombay v Holkar	Bombay	1944-45
1981-35 S Africa v England	Durban	1938-39
1929-39 NSW v S Australia	Sydney	1925-26
1911-34 NSW v Victoria	Sydney	1908-09
1905-40 Otago v Wellington	Dunedin	1923-24

The highest in England is:

1723-31 England v Australia	Leeds	1948

LOWEST INNINGS TOTALS

12	Oxford U v MCC	Oxford	1877
12	Northants v Glos	Gloucester	1907
13	Auckland v Canterbury	Auckland	1877-78
13	Notts v Yorks	Nottingham	1901
14	Surrey v Essex	Chelmsford	1983
15	MCC v Surrey	Lord's	1839
15	Victoria v MCC	Melbourne	1903-04
15	Northants v Yorks	Northampton	1908
15	Hants v Warwicks	Birmingham	1922
16	MCC v Surrey	Lord's	1872
16	Derbys v Notts	Nottingham	1879
16	Surrey v Notts	The Oval	1880
16	Warwicks v Kent	Tonbridge	1913
16	Trinidad v Barbados	Bridgetown	1941-42

FIRST-CLASS CRICKET RECORDS

16	Border v Natal (1st inns)	East London	1959-60
17	Gents of Kent v Gents of England	Lord's	1850
17	Glos v Australians	Cheltenham	1896
18	The B's v England	Lord's	1831
18	Kent v Sussex	Gravesend	1867
18	Tasmania v Victoria	Melbourne	1868-69
18	Australians v MCC	Lord's	1896
18	Border v Natal (2nd inns)	East London	1959-60
19	Sussex v Surrey	Godalming	1830
19	Sussex v Notts	Hove	1873
19	MCC v Australians	Lord's	1878
19	Wellington v Nelson	Nelson	1885-86

LOWEST MATCH AGGREGATES BY ONE TEAM

34 (16 & 18) Border v Natal	East London	1959-60
42 (27 & 15) Northants v Yorks	Northampton	1908
47 (12 & 35) Oxford U v MCC	Oxford	1877
51 (23 & 28) Jammu & Kashmir v Delhi	Srinagar	1960-61
52 (33 & 19) MCC v Australians	Lord's	1878
53 (18 & 35) The B's v England	Lord's	1831
53 (23 & 30) Kent v England	Bromley	1840
55 (22 & 33) Demerara v Barbados	Bridgetown	1864-65
55 (36 & 19) Wellington v Nelson	Nelson	1885-86

LOWEST MATCH AGGREGATES

Completed Matches (ie not drawn)

Runs-Wkts

105-31	MCC v Australians	Lord's	1878
134-30	England v The B's	Lord's	1831
147-40	Kent v Sussex	Sevenoaks	1828
149-30	England v Kent	Lord's	1858
150-30	Cambridge Town v MCC	Chatteris	1832
151-30	Canterbury v Otago	Christchurch	1866-67
153-37	MCC v Sussex	Lord's	1843
153-31	Otago v Canterbury	Dunedin	1896-97
156-30	Nelson v Wellington	Nelson	1885-86
158-22	Surrey v Worcs	The Oval	1954
159-31	Nelson v Wellington	Nelson	1887-88

Matches In Which 40 Wickets Fell

147-40	Kent v Sussex	Sevenoaks	1828
183-40	Nelson v Wellington	Nelson	1883-84
184-40	Fast Bowlers v Slow Bowlers	Lord's	1849
191-40	Oxford U v Australians	Oxford	1886

FIRST-CLASS CRICKET RECORDS

LARGEST MARGINS OF VICTORY

Largest Innings Victories

Inns & 851 Railways (910-6d) v Dera Ismail Khan	Lahore	1964-65
Inns & 666 Victoria (1059) v Tasmania	Melbourne	1922-23
Inns & 656 Victoria (1107) v NSW	Melbourne	1926-27
Inns & 605 NSW (918) v S Australia	Sydney	1900-01
Inns & 579 England (903-7d) v Australia	The Oval	1938
Inns & 575 Sind (951-7d) v Baluchistan	Karachi	1973-74
Inns & 527 NSW (713) v S Australia	Adelaide	1908-09
Inns & 517 Australians (675) v Notts	Nottingham	1921

Largest Victories By Runs Margins

685 NSW (235 & 761-8d) v Queensland	Sydney	1929-30
675 England (521 & 342-8d) v Australia	Brisbane	1928-29
638 NSW (304 & 770) v S Australia	Adelaide	1920-21
625 Sargodha (376 & 416) v Lahore MC	Faisalabad	1978-79
609 MC Bank (575 & 282-0d) v WAPDA	Hyderabad	1977-78
571 Victoria (304 & 649) v S Australia	Adelaide	1926-27
562 Australia (701 & 327) v England	The Oval	1934
550 Victoria (295 & 521) v Tasmania	Launceston	1913-14

VICTORY WITHOUT LOSING A WICKET

Lancs (166-0d & 66-0) bt Leics (108 & 122)	Manchester	1956
Karachi (277-0d) bt Sind (92 & 108)	Karachi	1957-58
Railways (236-0d & 16-0) bt Jammu & Kashmir (92 & 159)	Srinagar	1960-61
Karnataka (451-0d) bt Kerala (141 & 124)	Chickmagalur	1977-78

TIED MATCHES (SINCE 1945)

Southern Punjab v Baroda	Patiala	1945-46
Essex v Northants	Ilford	1947
Hants v Lancs	Bournemouth	1947
Hants v Kent	Southampton	1950
Sussex v Warwicks	Hove	1952
Essex v Lancs	Brentwood	1952
Northants v Middx	Peterborough	1953

Yorks v Leics	Huddersfield	1954
Sussex v Hants	Eastbourne	1955
Victoria v NSW	Melbourne	1956-57
TN Pearce's XI v New Zealanders	Scarborough	1958
Essex v Glos	Leyton	1959
Australia v West Indies	Brisbane	1960-61
The only instance in Test matches		
Bahawalpur v Lahore B	Bahawalpur	1961-62
Hants v Middx	Portsmouth	1967
England XI v England U-25 XI	Scarborough	1968
Yorks v Middx	Bradford	1973
Sussex v Essex	Hove	1974
S Australia v Queensland	Adelaide	1976-77
Central Districts v England XI	New Plymouth	1977-78
Peshawar v Allied Bank	Peshawar	1979-80
Victoria v New Zealanders	Melbourne	1982-83

MATCHES COMPLETED IN ONE DAY (SINCE 1945)

Derby v Somerset	Chesterfield	11 June 1947
Lancs v Sussex	Manchester	12 July 1950
Surrey v Warwicks	The Oval	16 May 1953
Somerset v Lancs	Bath	6 June 1953
Kent v Worcs	Tunbridge Wells	15 June 1960

FEWEST RUNS IN A FULL DAY'S PLAY

95 Australia (80) v Pakistan (15-2)	Karachi	1956-57
104 Pakistan (0-0 to 104-5) v Australia	Karachi	1959-60
105 Queensland (30-1 to 135-5) v MCC	Brisbane	1958-59
106 England (92-2 to 198) v Australia	Brisbane	1958-59
107 Pakistan XI (66-0 to 173-1) v MCC	Lahore	1955-56
110 Combined XI (159-2 to 260) v MCC (9-1)	Perth	1958-59
112 Sussex (112-7) v MCC	Lord's	1837
112 Australia (138-6 to 187) v Pakistan (63-1)	Karachi	1956-57
117 India (117-5) v Australia	Madras	1956-57

MOST RUNS IN A DAY

By One Team

R W

721 10	Australians (721) v Essex	Southend	1948
651 2	West Indians (682-2d) v Leics	Leicester	1950
649 8	NSW (752-8d) v Otago	Dunedin	1923-24
645 4	Surrey (742) v Hants	The Oval	1909

FIRST-CLASS CRICKET RECORDS

By Both Teams

R	W			
685	23	North (169-8d & 255-7) v South (261-8d)	Blackpool	1961
666	6	Northants (59-2) v Surrey (607-4)	Northampton	1920
663	6	Leics (160-2) v Middx (503-4)	Leicester	1947
649	11	Hants (570-8) v Somerset (79-3)	Taunton	1901
647	16	Sussex (115) v Surrey (532-6d)	The Oval	1919

The following instances occurred during two-day first-class matches in South Africa where the hours of play were extended.

R	W			
661	20	Griqualand West (460) v Border (201)	Kimberley	1920-21
645	16	Transvaal (450-9) v OFS (195-7)	Johannesburg	1920-21

FASTEST INNINGS

The following innings were scored at a rate of at least 125 runs per 100 balls (qualification: 200 runs)

Runs per 100 balls		Opponents		
156	Kent (219-2)	Gloucs	Dover	1937
132	Notts (279-1)	Leics	Nottingham	1949
127	Yorks (218-5)	Sussex	Hove	1959
127	Victoria (237-6)	Queensland	Brisbane	1963-64
125	Karachi (219-3)	Quetta	Karachi	1962-63

BATSMEN'S MATCHES

Qualification: 1200 runs, average 75 per wicket

Av			
189	Cambridge U (594-4d) v West Indies (730-3)	Cambridge	1950
95	Gloucs (383-3c & 404-4d) v Warwicks (438-5c & 105-2)	Bristol	1979
89	Worcs (380 & 344-2) v Leics (701-4d)	Worcester	1906
82	Maharashtra (624-5d) v Rajasthan (604)	Poona	1970-71
81	Leics (609-8d) v Sussex (686-8)	Leicester	1900
81	Yorks (344-3d & 321-2d) v Gloucs (321-6c & 235-4)	Leeds	1976

FIRST-CLASS CRICKET RECORDS

78	Karnataka (705) v Delhi (707-8)	Delhi	1981-82
75	Gloucs (643-5d) v Notts (467 & 168-2)	Bristol	1946
75	Notts (420) v West Indians (489-3d & 298-3)	Nottingham	1957

MOST HUNDREDS IN AN INNINGS

Six

Holkar (912-8d) v Mysore   Indore   1945-46
KV Bhandarkar 142, CT Sarwate 101,
MM Jagdale 164, CK Nayudu 101,
BB Nimbalkar 172, R Pratap Singh 100

MOST FIFTIES IN AN INNINGS

Eight

Australians (843) v Oxford &
  Cambridge U Past & Present   Portsmouth   1893
JJ Lyons 51, AC Bannerman 133,
GHS Trott 61, H Graham 83, W Bruce 191,
H Trumble 105, CTB Turner 66, WF Giffen 62

MOST EXTRAS IN AN INNINGS

Ext	B	LB	W	NB			
74	54	16	1	3	Demerara v W Shepherd's XI	Georgetown	1909-10
73	48	23	2	0	Northants v Kent	Northampton	1955
70	24	0	46	0	Camb U v Oxford U	Lord's	1839
70	23	30	1	16	Habib Bank v National Bank	Lahore	1976-77

UNUSUAL DISMISSALS

Although there are ten ways in which a batsman can lose his wicket, three of them occur very rarely (handled the ball, hit the ball twice, and obstructing the field) and the tenth ('timed out', introduced in 1980) failed to claim a victim in its initial first-class season.

Handled The Ball (Since 1945)

AW Gilbertson	Otago v Auckland	Auckland	1952-53
WR Endean	S Africa v England	Cape Town	1956-57
PJP Burge	Queensland v NSW	Sydney	1958-59
Dildar Awan	Services v Lahore	Lahore	1959-60
Mahmood-ul-Hasan	Karachi U v Railways & Quetta	Karachi	1960-61
Ali Raza	Karachi Greens v Hyderabad	Karachi	1961-62

FIRST-CLASS CRICKET RECORDS

Mohammad Yusuf	Rawalpindi v Peshawar	Peshawar	1962-63
A Rees	Glamorgan v Middx	Lord's	1965
Pervez Akhtar	Multan v Karachi Greens	Sahiwal	1971-72
Javed Mirza	Railways v Punjab	Lahore	1972-73
RG Pollock	E Province v W Province	Cape Town	1973-74
CI Dey	N Transvaal v OFS	Bloemfontein	1973-74
Nasir Valika	Karachi Whites v National Bank	Karachi	1974-75
Haji Yousuf	National Bank v Railways	Lahore	1974-75
Masood-ul-Hasan	PIA v National Bank B	Lyallpur	1975-76
DK Pearse	Natal v W Province	Cape Town	1978-79
AMJ Hilditch	Australia v Pakistan	Perth	1978-79
Musleh Uddin	Railways v Lahore	Lahore	1979-80
Mohsin Khan	Pakistan v Australia	Karachi	1982-83

Hit The Ball Twice (Since 1945)

AP Binns	Jamaica v British Guiana	Georgetown	1956-57
K Bavanna	Andhra v Mysore	Guntur	1963-64
Zaheer Abbas	PIA v Karachi Blues	Karachi	1969-70

The last instance in England:

JH King	Leics v Surrey	The Oval	1906

Obstructing The Field (Since 1945)

L Hutton	England v S Africa	The Oval	1951
JA Hayes	Canterbury v Central Districts	Christchurch	1954-55
DD Deshpande	Madhya Pradesh v Uttar Pradesh	Benares	1956-57
M Mehra	Railways v Delhi	Delhi	1959-60
K Ibadulla	Warwicks v Hants	Coventry	1963
Kaiser	Dera Ismail Khan v Railways	Lahore	1964-65
Qasim Feroze	Bahawalpur v Universities	Lahore	1974-75
T Quirk	Northern Transvaal v Border	East London	1978-79

South Africa's Graeme Pollock, whose career Test average of 60.97 (23 Tests) is second only to Bradman's record.

FIRST-CLASS CRICKET RECORDS

INDIVIDUAL RECORDS — BATTING

HIGHEST INDIVIDUAL INNINGS

499	Hanif Mohd.	Karachi v Bahawalpur	Karachi	1958-59
452*	DG Bradman	NSW v Queensland	Sydney	1929-30
443*	BB Nimbalkar	Maharashtra v Kathiawar	Poona	1948-49
437	WH Ponsford	Victoria v Queensland	Melbourne	1927-28
429	WH Ponsford	Victoria v Tasmania	Melbourne	1922-23
428	Aftab Baloch	Sind v Baluchistan	Karachi	1973-74
424	AC MacLaren	Lancs v Somerset	Taunton	1895
385	B Sutcliffe	Otago v Canterbury	Christchurch	1952-53
383	CW Gregory	NSW v Queensland	Brisbane	1906-07
369	DG Bradman	S Australia v Tasmania	Adelaide	1935-36
365*	C Hill	S Australia v NSW	Adelaide	1900-01
365*	G St A Sobers	W Indies v Pakistan	Kingston	1957-58
364	L Hutton	England v Australia	The Oval	1938
359*	VM Merchant	Bombay v Maharashtra	Bombay	1943-44
359	RB Simpson	NSW v Queensland	Brisbane	1963-64
357*	R Abel	Surrey v Somerset	Oval	1899
357	DG Bradman	S Australia v Victoria	Melbourne	1935-36
356	BA Richards	S Australia v W Australia	Perth	1970-71
355	B Sutcliffe	Otago v Auckland	Dunedin	1949-50
352	WH Ponsford	Victoria v NSW	Melbourne	1926-27
350	Rashid Israr	Habib Bank v National Bank	Lahore	1976-77
345	CG Macartney	Australians v Notts	Nottingham	1921
344*	GA Headley	Jamaica v Lord Tennyson's XI	Kingston	1931-32
344	WG Grace	MCC v Kent	Canterbury	1876
343*	PA Perrin	Essex v Derbys	Chesterfield	1904
341	GH Hirst	Yorks v Leics	Leicester	1905
340*	DG Bradman	NSW v Victoria	Sydney	1928-29
340	SM Gavaskar	Bombay v Bengal	Bombay	1981-82
338*	RC Blunt	Otago v Canterbury	Christchurch	1931-32
338	WW Read	Surrey v Oxford U	The Oval	1888
337*	Pervez Akhtar	Railways v Dera Ismail Khan	Lahore	1964-65
337	Hanif Mohd.	Pakistan v W Indies	Bridgetown	1957-58
336*	WR Hammond	England v NZ	Auckland	1932-33
336	WH Ponsford	Victoria v S Australia	Melbourne	1927-28
334	DG Bradman	Australia v England	Leeds	1930
333	KS Duleepsinhji	Sussex v Northants	Hove	1930
332	WH Ashdown	Kent v Essex	Brentwood	1934
331*	JDB Robertson	Middx v Worcs	Worcester	1949

76

FIRST-CLASS CRICKET RECORDS

HIGHEST MAIDEN HUNDREDS

337*	Pervez Akhtar	Railways v Dera Ismail Khan	Lahore	1964-65
324	Waheed Mirza	Karachi Whites v Quetta	Karachi	1976-77
292*	VT Trumper	NSW v Tasmania	Sydney	1898-99
290	WN Carson	Auckland v Otago	Dunedin	1936-37
290	Khalid Irtiza	United Bank v Multan	Karachi	1975-76
282	HL Collins	NSW v Tasmania	Hobart	1912-13
276	Altaf Shah	HBFC v Multan	Multan	1976-77
275	WA Farmer	Barbados v Jamaica	Bridgetown	1951-52
274	G Davidson	Derbys v Lancs	Manchester	1896
271	RI Maddocks	Victoria v Tasmania	Melbourne	1951-52
268	CRN Maxwell	Sir J. Cahn's XI v Leics	Nottingham	1935
268	HP Bayley	British Guiana v Barbados	Georgetown	1937-38
264	P Vaulkhard	Derbys v Notts	Nottingham	1946
264*	R Flockton	NSW v S Australia	Sydney	1959-60
262*	GL Wight	British Guiana v Barbados	Georgetown	1951-52
261*	SSL Steyn	Western Province v Border	Cape Town	1929-30
261	IR Redpath	Victoria v Queensland	Melbourne	1962-63
253	LS Birkett	Trinidad v British Guiana	Georgetown	1929-30

MOST DOUBLE HUNDREDS IN A SEASON

Six
DG Bradman 1930 334 254 252* 236 232 205*

Five
KS Ranjitsinhji 1900 275 222 220 215* 202
E de C Weekes 1950 232 304* 279 246* 200*

Four
CB Fry 1901 244 241 219* 209
EH Hendren 1929-30 254* 223* 211* 205*
WR Hammond 1933 264 239 231 206
WR Hammond 1934 302* 290 265* 217
VM Merchant 1944-45 221* 217 278 201
GM Turner 1971-72 202 223* 259 259

DOUBLE HUNDRED IN EACH INNINGS OF A MATCH

AE Fagg 244 202* Kent v Essex Colchester 1938

HUNDREDS BY NUMBER ELEVEN BATSMEN

163	TPB Smith	Essex v Derbys	Chesterfield	1947
126	WC Smith	MCC v Barbados	Bridgetown	1912-13

FIRST-CLASS CRICKET RECORDS

121	SN Banerjee	Indians v Surrey	The Oval	1946

He added 249 for the last wicket with the number 10, CT Sarwate who made 124*—the only instance of numbers 10 and 11 scoring centuries in the same innings.

115*	GB Stevenson	Yorks v Warwicks	Birmingham	1982
112*	A Fielder	Kent v Worcs	Stourbridge	1909
106*	TJ Hastings	Victoria v S Australia	Melbourne	1902-03
101	AER Gilligan	Cambridge U v Sussex	Hove	1919
100*	Ahsan-ul-Haq	Muslims v Sikhs	Lahore	1923-24

HIGHEST INNINGS ON DEBUT

240	WFE Marx	Transvaal v Griqualand West	Johannesburg	1920-21
232*	SJE Loxton	Victoria v Queensland	Melbourne	1946-47
230	GR Viswanath	Mysore v Andhra	Vijayawada	1967-68
227	T Marsden	Sheffield & Leicester v Nottingham	Sheffield	1826
215*	GHG Doggart	Cambridge U v Lancs	Cambridge	1948
207	NF Callaway	NSW v Queensland	Sydney	1914-15
202	J Hallebone	Victoria v Tasmania	Melbourne	1951-52
200*	A Maynard	Trinidad v MCC	Port-of-Spain	1934-35

HUNDRED IN ONLY FIRST-CLASS MATCH

NF Callaway	207	NSW v Queensland	Sydney	1914-15
SE Wootton	105	Victoria v Tasmania	Hobart	1923-24
HHE Grangel	108	Victoria v Tasmania	Melbourne	1935-36
RP Hammond-Chambers-Bornis	101	Combined Services v New Zealanders	Portsmouth	1937
MN Harbottle	56	Army v Oxford U	Camberley	1938
JR Gill	06	Ireland v MCC	Dublin	1948
Laheji	144	Saurashtra v Maharashtra	Rajkot	1954-55
JB Turner	106	Minor Counties v Pakistanis	Jesmond	1974
JS Johnson	146*	Minor Counties v Indians	Wellington	1979

MOST RUNS ADDED DURING A BATSMAN'S INNINGS

The following batsmen were at the wicket whilst over 700 runs were added during an innings in a first-class match. R Abel carried his bat through the innings when setting the record.

811	R Abel (357*)	Surrey v Somerset	The Oval	1899
801	WH Ponsford (429)	Victoria v Tasmania	Melbourne	1922-23
792	AC MacLaren (424)	Lancs v Somerset	Taunton	1895

FIRST-CLASS CRICKET RECORDS

792	WH Ponsford (437)	Victoria v Queensland	Melbourne	1927-28
772	Hanif Mohd. (499)	Karachi v Bahawalpur	Karachi	1958-59
770	L Hutton (364)	England v Australia	The Oval	1938
745	BB Nimbalkar (443*)	Maharashtra v Kathiawar	Poona	1948-49
739	DG Bradman (452*)	NSW v Queensland	Sydney	1929-30
720	A Sandham (325)	England v W Indies	Kingston	1929-30
702	GA Headley (344*)	Jamaica v Lord Tennyson's XI	Kingston	1931-32

HUNDRED IN EACH INNINGS OF A MATCH

Most Instances:
Eight
Zaheer Abbas for Gloucestershire (6) and PIA (2)   1976-82

On The Same Day
KS Ranjitsinhji   Sussex v Yorks   Hove   1896

Carrying Bat Through Both Completed Innings
CJB Wood   Leics v Yorks   Bradford   1911

Twice In Successive Matches
TW Hayward for Surrey   1906
DW Hookes for S Australia   1976-77

On First-Class Debut
AR Morris   NSW v Queensland   Sydney   1940-41
NJ Contractor   Gujarat v Baroda   Baroda   1952-53
Aamir Malik   Lahore v Railways   Lahore   1979-80

MOST HUNDREDS IN CONSECUTIVE INNINGS

Six
CB Fry   for Sussex (5) and Rest of England   1901
DG Bradman   for S Australia (5) and DG Bradman's XI   1938-39
MJ Procter   for Rhodesia   1970-71

MOST FIFTIES IN CONSECUTIVE INNINGS

Ten
GE Tyldesley   for Lancs (8), England and Players   1926
DG Bradman   for Australia (4) and Australians (6) 1947-48 & 1948

MOST RUNS BEFORE BEING DISMISSED

709   KC Ibrahim   218*-36*-234*-77*-144   Bombay   1947-48

FIRST-CLASS CRICKET RECORDS

MOST RUNS IN A MATCH

499 (499)	Hanif Mohammad	Karachi v Bahawalpur	Karachi	1958-59
455 (3 & 452*)	DG Bradman	NSW v Queensland	Sydney	1929-30
446 (244 & 202*)	AE Fagg	Kent v Essex	Colchester	1938
443 (443*)	BB Nimbalkar	Maharashtra v Kathiawar	Poona	1948-49
437 (437)	WH Ponsford	Victoria v Queensland	Melbourne	1927-28
429 (429)	WH Ponsford	Victoria v Tasmania	Melbourne	1922-23
428 (428)	Aftab Baloch	Sind v Baluchistan	Karachi	1973-74
424 (424)	AC MacLaren	Lancs v Somerset	Taunton	1895
402 (157* & 245)	WW Armstrong	Victoria v S Australia	Melbourne	1920-21

The highest match aggregate in Test cricket is 380 by GS Chappell (247* & 133) for Australia v New Zealand at Wellington in 1973-74

CARRYING BAT THROUGH A COMPLETED INNINGS

A feat achieved by an opening batsman when he bats throughout a completed innings in which all ten of his partners are dismissed.

In Both Innings Of A Match

H Jupp	Surrey v Yorks	The Oval	1874
S Kinneir	Warwicks v Leics	Leicester	1907
CJB Wood	Leics v Yorks	Bradford	1911
VM Merchant	Indians v Lancs	Liverpool	1936

Highest Score
R Abel 357* Surrey v Somerset   The Oval 1899

Surrey's total of 811 is the highest through which a player has carried his bat.

FAST SCORING

Fastest Hundred
Min

35	PGH Fender	Surrey v Northants	Northampton 1920
35	SJ O'Shaughnessy	Lancs v Leics	Manchester 1983

Facing full-tosses and long-hops from two non-bowlers.

Fastest Fifty
Min

8	CC Inman	Leics v Notts	Nottingham 1965

Facing full-tosses from a non-bowler

FIRST-CLASS CRICKET RECORDS

Fastest Double Hundred
Min

120	GL Jessop	Gloucs v Sussex	Hove	1903
120	CH Lloyd	West Indians v Glamorgan	Swansea	1976

Fastest Triple Hundred
Min

181	DCS Compton	MCC v NE Transvaal	Benoni	1948-49

Most Runs Before Lunch

197	WR Endean	Transvaal v OFS	Johannesburg	1954-55

Most Runs From One Ball
   Batsman   **Bowler**

10	AN Hornby	J Street	Lancs v Surrey	The Oval	1873
10	SH Wood	CJ Burnup	Derbys v MCC	Lord's	1900

Recorded under the 'net' system of scoring in trial use in 1900

The most runs from one ball, all-run and without the benefit of overthrows or penalties under Law 41.1, are:
   Batsman   **Bowler**

9 Hon FGB Ponsonby — MCC v Cambridge U Cambridge 1842

Clive Lloyd, who scored a record-equalling double hundred in two hours for the West Indians.

Denis Compton hit a triple hundred in a record three hours one minute for MCC.

FIRST-CLASS CRICKET RECORDS

Most Runs From One Over
Six-Ball Overs

	Batsman	Bowler		
36 (666666)	G St A Sobers	MA Nash	Notts v Glamorgan Swansea	1968
34 (646666)	FC Hayes	MA Nash	Lancs v Glamorgan Swansea	1977
34 (46604446)	EB Alletson	EH Killick	Notts v Sussex Hove	1911
Including two no-balls				

Eight-Ball Overs

	Batsman	Bowler		
34 (40446664)	RM Edwards	MC Carew	Governor-General's XI v West Indians Auckland	1968-69

Most Sixes In An Innings

15 JR Reid   Wellington v Northern Districts   Wellington   1962-63

Most Sixes In A Match

17 WJ Stewart   Warwicks v Lancs   Blackpool   1959
His innings of 155 and 125 included 10 sixes and 7 sixes respectively.

Most Sixes In A Season

72	AW Wellard	Somerset	1935
57	AW Wellard	Somerset	1936
57	AW Wellard	Somerset	1938
51	AW Wellard	Somerset	1933
49	JH Edrich	Surrey	1965
48	AW Carr	Notts	1925
46	F Barratt	Notts	1928
46	HT Bartlett	Sussex	1938

Most Runs From Strokes Worth Four Or More In An Innings

R   6s   4s

R	6s	4s				
272	-	68	PA Perrin (343*)	Essex v Derbys	Chesterfield	1904
262	1	64	AC MacLaren (424)	Lancs v Somerset	Taunton	1895
256	-	64	Hanif Mohd. (499)	Karachi v Bahawalpur	Karachi	1958-59
238	5	52	JH Edrich (310*)	England v NZ	Leeds	1965
230	15	35	JR Reid (296)	Wellington v N Districts	Wellington	1962-63

FIRST-CLASS CRICKET RECORDS

3000 RUNS IN A SEASON

	Season	I	NO	HS	Runs	Avge	100
DCS Compton	1947	50	8	246	3816	90.85	18
WJ Edrich	1947	52	8	267*	3539	80.43	12
TW Hayward	1906	61	8	219	3518	66.37	13
L Hutton	1949	56	6	269*	3429	68.58	12
FE Woolley	1928	59	4	198	3352	60.94	12
H Sutcliffe	1932	52	7	313	3336	74.13	14
WR Hammond	1933	54	5	264	3323	67.81	13
EH Hendren	1928	54	7	209*	3311	70.44	13
R Abel	1901	68	8	247	3309	55.15	7
WR Hammond	1937	55	5	217	3252	65.04	13
MJK Smith	1959	67	11	200*	3245	57.94	8
EH Hendren	1933	65	9	301*	3186	56.89	11
CP Mead	1921	52	6	280*	3179	69.10	10
TW Hayward	1904	63	5	203	3170	54.65	11
KS Ranjitsinhji	1899	58	8	197	3159	63.18	8
CB Fry	1901	43	3	244	3147	78.67	13
KS Ranjitsinhji	1900	40	5	275	3065	87.57	11
LEG Ames	1933	57	5	295	3058	58.80	9
JT Tyldesley	1901	60	5	221	3041	55.29	9
CP Mead	1928	50	10	180	3027	75.67	13
JB Hobbs	1925	48	5	266*	3024	70.32	16
GE Tyldesley	1928	48	10	242	3024	79.57	10
WE Alley	1961	64	11	221*	3019	56.96	11
WR Hammond	1938	42	2	271	3011	75.27	15
EH Hendren	1923	51	12	200*	3010	77.17	13
H Stucliffe	1931	42	11	230	3006	96.96	13
JH Parks	1937	63	4	168	3003	50.89	11
H Sutcliffe	1928	44	5	228	3002	76.97	13

MOST HUNDREDS IN A SEASON

18	DCS Compton	Middlesex	1947
16	JB Hobbs	Surrey	1925
15	WR Hammond	Gloucestershire	1938
14	H Sutcliffe	Yorkshire	1932
13	DG Bradman	Australians	1938
13	CB Fry	Sussex	1901
13	WR Hammond	Gloucestershire	1933
13	WR Hammond	Gloucestershire	1937
13	TW Hayward	Surrey	1906
13	EH Hendren	Middlesex	1923
13	EH Hendren	Middlesex	1927
13	EH Hendren	Middlesex	1928
13	CP Mead	Hampshire	1928
13	H Sutcliffe	Yorkshire	1928
13	H Sutcliffe	Yorkshire	1931
13	G Boycott	Yorkshire	1971

12	R Abel	Surrey	1900
12	KS Duleepsinhji	Sussex	1931
12	WJ Edrich	Middlesex	1947
12	WR Hammond	Gloucestershire	1927
12	JB Hobbs	Surrey	1928
12	L Hutton	Yorkshire	1939
12	L Hutton	Yorkshire	1949
12	JG Langridge	Sussex	1949
12	JDB Robertson	Middlesex	1947
12	FE Woolley	Kent	1928

HIGHEST BATTING AVERAGES IN AN ENGLISH SEASON

	Season	I	NO	HS	Runs	Avge	100
DG Bradman	1938	26	5	278	2429	115.66	13
G Boycott	1979	20	5	175*	1538	102.53	6
WA Johnston	1953	17	16	28*	102	102.00	-
G Boycott	1971	30	5	233	2503	100.12	13
DG Bradman	1930	36	6	334	2960	98.66	10
H Sutcliffe	1931	42	11	230	3006	96.96	13
RM Poore	1899	21	4	304	1551	91.23	7
DR Jardine	1927	14	3	147	1002	91.09	5
DCS Compton	1947	50	8	246	3816	90.85	18
GM Turner	1982	16	3	311*	1171	90.07	5

1000 RUNS IN A MONTH

May	Season	I	NO	HS	Runs	Avge
WG Grace	1895	10	1	288	1016	112.88
WR Hammond	1927	14	0	192	1042	74.42
C Hallows	1928	11	3	232	1000	125.00

June						
KS Ranjitsinhji	1899	15	2	197	1037	79.76
CB Fry	1901	11	2	244	1130	125.55
J Iremonger	1904	11	1	272	1010	101.00
CP Mead	1921	13	1	280*	1159	96.58
EH Hendren	1925	12	2	240	1122	112.20
JB Hobbs	1925	14	1	215	1112	85.53
P Holmes	1925	12	2	315*	1021	102.10
H Sutcliffe	1932	14	3	313	1193	108.45
L Hutton	1949	16	2	201	1294	92.42
Zaheer Abbos	1981	14	5	215*	1016	112.88

July						
KS Ranjitsinhji	1900	12	1	275	1059	96.27
D Denton	1912	14	2	221	1023	85.25

FIRST-CLASS CRICKET RECORDS

CP Mead	1923	13	6	222	1070	152.85
GE Tyldesley	1926	9	1	226	1024	128.00
AE Fagg	1938	15	1	244	1016	72.57
C Washbrook	1946	14	3	162	1079	98.09
WJ Edrich	1947	11	3	267*	1047	130.87
MJK Smith	1959	15	2	200*	1209	93.00

August

WG Grace	1871	11	0	268	1024	93.09
WG Grace	1876	11	1	344	1278	127.80
KS Ranjitsinhji	1899	14	1	161	1011	77.76
CB Fry	1901	12	1	209	1116	101.45
H Sutcliffe	1932	13	1	194	1006	83.83
M Leyland	1932	13	1	166	1013	84.41
EH Hendren	1933	18	2	222*	1110	69.37
WR Hammond	1933	13	3	264	1060	106.00
WW Keeton	1933	15	2	136*	1102	84.76
WR Hammond	1936	16	3	317	1281	98.53
EH Hendren	1936	14	0	156	1026	73.28
J Hardstaff jr	1937	11	1	266	1150	115.00
DCS Compton	1947	12	3	178	1039	115.44
L Hutton	1949	15	1	269*	1050	75.00

December

WH Ponsford	1927	5	0	437	1146	229.20

1000 RUNS BEFORE JUNE

Although only WG Grace, WR Hammond and C Hallows have scored 1000 runs within the month of May, four others have reached 1000 runs before the end of May with the aid of some innings in April—DG Bradman achieving this feat twice:

	Season	I	NO	HS	Runs	Avge
TW Hayward	1900	13	2	193	1074	97.63
DG Bradman	1930	11	4	262*	1001	143.00
DG Bradman	1938	9	2	278	1056	150.85
WJ Edrich	1938	15	3	245	1010	84.16
GM Turner	1973	18	5	153*	1018	78.30

PARTNERSHIP RECORDS: WORLD RECORD FOR EACH WICKET

1st	561	Waheed Mirza, Mansoor Akhtar	Karachi Whites v Quetta	Karachi	1976-77
2nd	465*	JA Jameson, RB Kanhai	Warwicks v Gloucs	Birmingham	1974
3rd	456	Khalid Irtiza, Aslam Ali	United Bank v Multan	Karachi	1975-76
4th	577	VS Hazare, Gul Mahomed	Baroda v Holkar	Baroda	1946-47

FIRST-CLASS CRICKET RECORDS

5th	405	SG Barnes, DG Bradman	Australia v England	Sydney	1946-47
6th	487*	GA Headley, CC Passailaigue	Jamaica v Ld Tennyson's XI	Kingston	1931-32
7th	347	D St E Atkinson, CC Depeiza	West Indies v Australia	Bridgetown	1954-55
8th	433	A Sims, VT Trumper	Australian XI v Canterbury	Christ-church	1913-14
9th	283	J Chapman, A Warren	Derbys v Warwicks	Blackwell	1910
10th	307	AF Kippax, JEH Hooker	NSW v Victoria	Melbourne	1928-29

INDIVIDUAL RECORDS — BOWLING

TEN WICKETS IN AN INNINGS (since 1945)

WE Hollies	Warwicks v Notts	Birmingham	1946
JM Sims	East v West	Kingston upon Thames	1948
JKR Graveney	Gloucs v Derbys	Chesterfield	1949
TE Bailey	Essex v Lancs	Clacton	1949
R Berry	Lancs v Worcs	Blackpool	1953
SP Gupte	Bombay v Pakistan Services & Bahawalpur	Bombay	1954-55
JC Laker	Surrey v Australians	The Oval	1956
K Smales	Notts v Gloucs	Stroud	1956
GAR Lock	Surrey v Kent	Blackheath	1956
JC Laker	England v Australia	Manchester	1956
PM Chatterjee	Bengal v Assam	Jorhat	1956-57
JD Bannister	Warwicks v Combined Services	Birmingham	1959
AJG Pearson	Cambridge U v Leics	Loughborough	1961
NI Thomson	Sussex v Warwicks	Worthing	1964
PJ Allan	Queensland v Victoria	Melbourne	1965-66
IJ Brayshaw	W Australia v Victoria	Perth	1967-68
Shahid Mahmood	Karachi Whites v Khairpur	Karachi	1969-70
EE Hemmings	International XI v West Indies XI	Kingston	1982-83

MOST WICKETS IN A MATCH

Nineteen

JC Laker	England v Australia	Manchester	1956

FIRST-CLASS CRICKET RECORDS

Seventeen

FP Fenner	Camb Town v Camb U	Cambridge	1844
W Mycroft	Derbys v Hants	Southampton 1876	
WG Grace	Gloucs v Notts	Cheltenham	1877
G Giffen	S Australia v Victoria	Adelaide	1885-86
CTB Turner	Australians v England XI	Hastings	1888
W Mead	Essex v Hants	Southampton 1895	
WP Howell	Australians v W Province	Cape Town	1902-03
W Brearley	Lancs v Somerset	Manchester	1905
C Blythe	Kent v Northants	Northampton 1907	
H Dean	Lancs v Yorks	Liverpool	1913
SF Barnes	England v S Africa	Johannesburg	1913-14
AP Freeman	Kent v Sussex	Hove	1922
FC Matthews	Notts v Northants	Nottingham	1923
CWL Parker	Gloucs v Essex	Gloucester	1925
GR Cox	Sussex v Warwicks	Horsham	1926
AP Freeman	Kent v Warwicks	Folkestone	1932
H Verity	Yorks v Essex	Leyton	1933
JC Clay	Glamorgan v Worcs	Swansea	1937
TWJ Goddard	Gloucs v Kent	Bristol	1939

MOST WICKETS IN A DAY

Seventeen

C Blythe	Kent v Northants	Northampton 1907	
H Verity	Yorks v Essex	Leyton	1933
TWJ Goddard	Gloucs v Kent	Bristol	1939

Sixteen

T Emmett	Yorks v Cambridgeshire	Hunslet, Leeds 1869	
AEE Vogler	E Province v Griqualand West	Johannesburg	1906-07
J Southerton	South v North	Lord's	1875
TG Wass	Notts v Lancs	Liverpool	1906
JC White	Somerset v Worcs	Bath	1919
TG Wass	Notts v Essex	Nottingham	1908

250 WICKETS IN A SEASON

	Season	Wkts	Avge
AP Freeman	1928	304	18.05
AP Freeman	1933	298	15.26
T Richardson	1895	290	14.37

FIRST-CLASS CRICKET RECORDS

CTB Turner	1888	283	11.68
AP Freeman	1931	276	15.60
AP Freeman	1930	275	16.84
T Richardson	1897	273	14.45
AP Freeman	1929	267	18.27
W Rhodes	1900	261	13.81
JT Hearne	1896	257	14.28
AP Freeman	1932	253	16.39
W Rhodes	1901	251	15.12

MOST RECENT INSTANCES OF 250, 200 and 150 WICKETS

250 wickets	AP Freeman	Kent	1933
200 wickets	GAR Lock	Surrey	1957
150 wickets	DL Underwood	Kent	1966

The highest aggregate of first-class wickets in a season since 1966 is 134 by MD Marshall (Hants) in 1982.

100 WICKETS IN A SEASON SINCE 1971

The feat of taking a hundred first-class wickets in a season was achieved every year from 1864 to 1971 inclusive, war years excepted. A drastic pruning of the County Championship fixtures to 20 matches per county in 1972 reduced the number of instances to only six in the next five seasons. No bowler reached this aggregate in 1972 or 1976. Subsequently the fixtures have been increased to 22 per county (1977-82) and 24 in 1983 when four bowlers achieved this total.

	Season	Overs	Runs	Wkts	Avge
BS Bedi	1973	864.2	1884	105	17.94
	1974	1085.3	2760	112	24.64
IT Botham	1978	605.2	1640	100	16.40
DR Doshi	1980	961.2	2700	101	26.73
JE Emburey	1983	935	1842	103	17.88
N Gifford	1983	1043.4	2393	104	23.00
RD Jackman	1980	746.2	1864	121	15.40
PG Lee	1973	740.3	1901	101	18.82
	1975	799.5	2067	112	18.45
JK Lever	1978	681.1	1610	106	15.18
	1979	700	1834	106	17.30
	1983	569	1726	106	16.28
MD Marshall	1982	822	2108	134	15.73
MJ Procter	1977	777.3	1967	109	18.04
AME Roberts	1974	727.4	1621	119	13.62
Sarfraz Nawaz	1975	728.4	2051	101	20.30
MWW Selvey	1978	743.5	1929	101	19.09
DL Underwood	1978	815.1	1594	110	14.49
	1979	799.2	1575	106	14.85
	1983	936.3	2044	106	19.28

FIRST-CLASS CRICKET RECORDS

MOST BALLS BOWLED IN A SEASON

12234 AP Freeman 1933 (298 wkts)

MOST RUNS CONCEDED IN A SEASON

5489 AP Freeman 1928 (304 wkts)

BOWLING TEN BATSMEN IN AN INNINGS

J Wisden   North v South   Lord's   1850

MOST RUNS CONCEDED IN AN INNINGS

362 AA Mailey NSW v Victoria Melbourne 1926-27

MOST BALLS BOWLED IN AN INNINGS

588 S Ramadhin West Indies v England Birmingham 1957

MOST RUNS CONCEDED IN A MATCH

428 CS Nayudu Holkar v Bombay Bombay 1944-45

MOST BALLS BOWLED IN A MATCH

917 CS Nayudu Holkar v Bombay Bombay 1944-45

FOUR WICKETS WITH CONSECUTIVE BALLS

J Wells	Kent v Sussex	Brighton	1862
G Ulyett	Lord Harris' XI v NSW	Sydney	1878-79
G Nash	Lancs v Somerset	Manchester	1882
JB Hide	Sussex v MCC	Lord's	1890
FJ Shacklock	Notts v Somerset	Nottingham	1893
AD Downes	Otago v Auckland	Dunedin	1893-94
F Martin	MCC v Derbys	Lord's	1895
AW Mold	Lancs v Notts	Nottingham	1895
W Brearley	†Lancs v Somerset	Manchester	1905
S Haigh	MCC v Army	Pretoria	1905-06
AE Trott	††Middx v Somerset	Lord's	1907
FA Tarrant	Middx v Gloucs	Bristol	1907
A Drake	Yorks v Derbys	Chesterfield	1914
SG Smith	Northants v Warwicks	Birmingham	1914
HA Peach	Surrey v Sussex	The Oval	1924
AF Borland	Natal v Griqualand West	Kimberley	1926-27
JEH Hooker	†NSW v Victoria	Sydney	1928-29
RK Tyldesley	†Lancs v Derbys	Derby	1929
RJ Crisp	Western Province v Griqualand West	Johannesburg	1931-32
RJ Crisp	Western Province v Natal	Durban	1933-34
AR Gover	Surrey v Worcs	Worcester	1935
WH Copson	Derbys v Warwicks	Derby	1937

FIRST-CLASS CRICKET RECORDS

WA Henderson	NE Transvaal v	Bloemfontein	
	Orange Free State		1937-38
F Ridgway	Kent v Derbys	Folkestone	1951
AK Walker	† Notts v Leics	Leicester	1956
SN Mohol	President's XI v		
	Combined XI	Poona	1965-66
PI Pocock	Surrey v Sussex	Eastbourne	1972

† Not all in the same innings.
††Trott achieved another hat-trick in the same innings of this, his benefit match.

HAT-TRICKS

Twice in same innings

AE Trott	Middx v Somerset	Lord's	1907
JS Rao	Services v N Punjab	Amritsar	1963-64

In both innings of a match

A Shaw	Notts v Gloucs	Nottingham	1884
TJ Matthews	Australia v South Africa	Manchester	1912
CWL Parker	Gloucs v Middx	Bristol	1924
RO Jenkins	Worcs v Surrey	Worcester	1949
Amin Lakhani	Universities & Youth XI v		
	Indians	Multan	1978-79

Most hat-tricks

7 DVP Wright
6 TWJ Goddard, CWL Parker
5 S Haigh, VWC Jupp, AEG Rhodes, FA Tarrant
4 RG Barlow, JT Hearne, JC Laker, GAR Lock, GG Macaulay,
  TJ Matthews, MJ Procter, T Richardson, FR Spofforth, FS Trueman
3 WM Bradley, HJ Butler, WH Copson, RJ Crisp, JWHT Douglas,
  JA Flavell, AP Freeman, G Giffen, K Higgs, A Hill,
  WA Humphreys, RD Jackman, RO Jenkins, AS Kennedy,
  W Lockwood, EA McDonald, TL Pritchard, JS Rao, A Shaw,
  JB Statham, MW Tate, H Trumble, D Wilson, GA Wilson.

INDIVIDUAL RECORDS — ALL-ROUND PERFORMANCES

THE INNINGS DOUBLE

Century and all ten wickets

VE Walker	England v Surrey	The Oval	1859
WG Grace	MCC v Oxford U	Oxford	1886
FA Tarrant	Maharaja of Cooch Behar's XI v		
	Lord Willingdon's XI	Poona	1918-19

FIRST-CLASS CRICKET RECORDS

THE MATCH DOUBLE

100 runs and ten wickets

This feat is comparatively rare, only 20 instances being achieved in English first-class cricket since 1945, the most recent by IA Greig for Sussex v Hampshire at Hove in 1981.

UNIQUE MATCH DOUBLES

Hundred in each innings and five wickets twice

| **GH Hirst** | Yorks v Somerset | Bath | 1906 |

Hundred in each innings and ten wickets

| **BJT Bosanquet** | Middx v Sussex | Lord's | 1905 |

200 runs and 16 wickets

| **G Giffen** | S Australia v Victoria | Adelaide | 1891-92 |

HUNDRED AND A HAT-TRICK

G Giffen	Australians v Lancs	Manchester	1884
WE Roller	Surrey v Sussex	The Oval	1885
WB Burns	Worcs v Gloucs	Worcester	1913
VWC Jupp	Sussex v Essex	Colchester	1921
RES Wyatt	MCC v Ceylon	Colombo	1926-27
LN Constantine	West Indians v Northants	Northampton	1928
DE Davies	Glamorgan v Leics	Leicester	1937
VM Merchant	Dr CR Pereira's XI v Sir H Mehta's XI	Bombay	1946-47
MJ Procter	Gloucs v Essex	Westcliff	1972
MJ Procter	Gloucs v Leics	Bristol	*1979

THE SEASON DOUBLE

The double of 1000 runs and 100 wickets in a first-class season was first achieved in 1874 by WG Grace. He repeated this performance in each of the next four seasons but it was not until 1882 that another player, CT Studd, emulated him. Apart from the war years, only two seasons (1951 and 1958) between 1895 and 1967 inclusive failed to produce at least one instance of a player doing the double. Mainly because of the reduced first-class fixtures list, no player has achieved this feat since FJ Titmus in 1967.

In 1949 DB Close of Yorkshire, aged 18, became the youngest player to do the double and the only one to achieve it in the season of his first appearance in first-class cricket.

VWC Jupp (Sussex and Northants) and FR Brown (Surrey and Northants) are alone in achieving the double for two counties.

FIRST-CLASS CRICKET RECORDS

Outstanding doubles

	Season	Runs	Wkts
2000 runs and 200 wickets			
GH Hirst	1906	2385	208
3000 runs and 100 wickets			
JH Parks	1937	3003	101
1000 runs and 200 wickets			
AE Trott	1899	1175	239
AE Trott	1900	1337	211
AS Kennedy	1922	1129	205
MW Tate	1923	1168	219
MW Tate	1924	1419	205
MW Tate	1925	1290	228
2000 runs and 100 wickets			
WG Grace	1876	2622	129
CL Townsend	1899	2440	101
GL Jessop	1900	2210	104
GH Irst	1904	2501	132
GH Hirst	1905	2266	110
W Rhodes	1909	2094	141
W Rhodes	1911	2261	117
FA Tarrant	1911	2030	111
JW Hearne	1913	2036	124
JW Hearne	1914	2116	123
FE Woolley	1914	2272	125
JW Hearne	1920	2148	142
VWC Jupp	1921	2169	121
FE Woolley	1921	2101	167
FE Woolley	1922	2022	163
FE Woolley	1923	2091	101
LF Townsend	1933	2268	100
DE Davies	1937	2012	103
James Langridge	1937	2082	101
TE Bailey	1959	2011	100

Fastest doubles

GH Hirst (Yorks) completed the double in only 16 matches, on 28 June 1906.

Most doubles

16	W Rhodes
14	GH Hirst
10	VWC Jupp
9	WE Astill
8	TE Bailey, MS Nichols, AE Relf, FA Tarrant, MW Tate, FJ Titmus and FE Woolley.

FIRST-CLASS CRICKET RECORDS

THE WICKET-KEEPER'S DOUBLE

1000 runs and 100 dismissals

		Season	Runs	Dis
LEG Ames	Kent	1928	1919	121
LEG Ames	Kent	1929	1795	127
LEG Ames	Kent	1932	2482	100
JT Murray	Middx	1957	1025	104

INDIVIDUAL RECORDS — WICKET-KEEPING

MOST DISMISSALS IN AN INNINGS

Eight

ATW Grout	Queensland v W Australia	Brisbane	1959-60

All caught—a double world record

Seven

KV Andrew	Northants v Lancs	Manchester	1962
DL Bairstow	Yorks v Derbys	Scarborough	1982
S Benjamin	Central Zone v N Zone	Bombay	1973-74
J Brown	Scotland v Ireland	Dublin	1957
W Farrimond	Lancs v Kent	Manchester	1930
EW Jones	Glamorgan v Cambridge U	Cambridge	1970
N Kirsten	Border v Rhodesia	East London	1959-60
A Long	Surrey v Sussex	Hove	1964
JA Maclean	Queensland v Victoria	Melbourne	1977-78
WFF Price	Middx v Yorks	Lord's	1937
RA Saggers	NSW v Combined XI	Brisbane	1940-41
RM Schofield	Central Districts v Wellington	Wellington	1964-65
Shahid Israr	Karachi Whites v Quetta	Karachi	1976-77
EJ Smith	Warwicks v Derbys	Birmingham	1926
MS Smith	Natal v Border	East London	1959-60
HB Taber	NSW v S Australia	Adelaide	1968-69
D Tallon	Queensland v Victoria	Brisbane	1938-39
Taslim Arif	National Bank v Punjab	Lahore	1978-79
RW Taylor (3)	Derbys v Glamorgan	Derby	1966
	Derbys v Yorks	Chesterfield	1975
	England v India	Bombay	1979-80
Wasim Bari	Pakistan v New Zealand	Auckland	1978-79
H Yarnold †	Worcs v Scotland	Broughty Ferry	1951

† including six stumpings—the world record

FIRST-CLASS CRICKET RECORDS

MOST DISMISSALS IN A MATCH

Twelve

E Pooley	Surrey v Sussex	The Oval	1868
HB Taber	NSW v S Australia	Adelaide	1968-69
D Tallon	Queensland v NSW	Sydney	1938-39

Eleven

DL Bairstow	Yorks v Derbys	Scarborough	1982
A Long	Surrey v Sussex	Hove	1964
RW Marsh	W Australia v Victoria	Perth	1975-76

MOST DISMISSALS IN A SEASON

	Season	Total	Ct	St
LEG Ames	1929	127	79	48
LEG Ames	1928	121	69	52
H Yarnold	1949	110	63	47
G Duckworth	1928	107	77	30
JG Binks	1960	107	96	11
JT Murray	1957	104	82	22
FH Huish	1913	102	70	32
JT Murray	1960	102	95	7
R Booth	1960	101	85	16
FH Huish	1911	100	62	38
LEG Ames	1932	100	36	64
R Booth	1964	100	91	9

Most catches in a season 96 JG Binks 1960
Most stumpings in a season 64 LEG Ames 1932

INDIVIDUAL RECORDS — FIELDING

MOST CATCHES IN AN INNINGS

Seven

AS Brown	Gloucs v Notts	Nottingham	1966
MJ Stewart	Surrey v Northants	Northampton	1957

FIRST-CLASS CRICKET RECORDS

Six

M Bissex	Gloucs v Sussex	Hove	1968
RG Broadbent	Worcs v Glamorgan	Stourbridge	1960
JD Clay	Notts v Derbys	Nottingham	1957
LM Dean	Europeans v Parsees	Poona	1898-99
KJ Grieves	Lancs v Sussex	Manchester	1951
G Griffith	Surrey v Gents of South	The Oval	1863
WR Hammond (2)	Gloucs v Surrey	Cheltenham	1928
	Gloucs v Notts	Bristol	1933
SE Leary	Kent v Cambridge U	Cambridge	1958
EP Robinson	Yorks v Leics	Bradford	1938
J Seymour	Kent v South Africans	Canterbury	1904
JF Sheppard	Queensland v NSW	Brisbane	1914-15
MJK Smith	Warwicks v Leics	Hinckley	1962
FA Tarrant	Middx v Essex	Leyton	1906
RK Tyldesley	Lancs v Hants	Liverpool	1921
AJ Webbe	Gentlemen v Players	Lord's	1877

MOST CATCHES IN A MATCH

Ten

WR Hammond	Gloucs v Surrey	Cheltenham	1928

Eight

AH Bakewell	Northants v Essex	Leyton	1928
WB Burns	Worcs v Yorks	Bradford	1907
KJ Grieves	Lancs v Sussex	Manchester	1951
WR Hammond	Gloucs v Worcs	Cheltenham	1932
GAR Lock	Surrey v Warwicks	The Oval	1957
Javed Miandad	Habib Bank v Universities	Lahore	1977-78
CA Milton	Gloucs v Sussex	Hove	1952
JM Prodger	Kent v Gloucs	Cheltenham	1961
PM Walker	Glamorgan v Derbys	Swansea	1970

MOST CATCHES IN A SEASON

78	**WR Hammond**	Gloucs	1928
77	**MJ Stewart**	Surrey	1957
73	**PM Walker**	Glamorgan	1961
71	**PJ Sharpe**	Yorks	1962
70	**J Tunnicliffe**	Yorks	1901
69	**JG Langridge**	Sussex	1955
69	**PM Walker**	Glamorgan	1960
65	**J Tunnicliffe**	Yorks	1895
65	**WR Hammond**	Gloucs	1925
65	**PW Walker**	Glamorgan	1959
65	**DW Richardson**	Worcs	1961

FIRST-CLASS CRICKET RECORDS

CAREER RECORDS

1971 denotes the overseas season of 1971-72

BATTING: LEADING AGGREGATES (30,000 RUNS)

	Career	I	NO	HS	Runs	Avge
JB Hobbs	1905-1934	1315	106	316*	61237	50.65
FE Woolley	1906-1938	1530	84	305*	58959	40.77
EH Hendren	1907-1938	1300	166	301*	57611	50.80
CP Mead	1905-1936	1340	185	280*	55061	47.67
WG Grace	1865-1908	1478	104	344	54211	39.45
WR Hammond	1920-1951	1005	104	336*	50551	56.10
H Sutcliffe	1919-1945	1088	123	313	50138	51.95
TW Graveney	1948-1971	1223	159	258	47793	44.91
G Boycott	1962-1983	925	139	261*	44210	56.24
TW Hayward	1893-1914	1138	96	315*	43551	41.79
MC Cowdrey	1950-1976	1130	134	307	42719	42.89
A Sandham	1911-1937	1000	79	325	41284	44.82
L Hutton	1934-1960	814	91	364	40140	55.51
MJK Smith	1951-1975	1091	139	204	39832	41.84
W Rhodes	1898-1930	1527	237	267*	39763	30.82
JH Edrich	1956-1978	979	104	310*	39790	45.47
RES Wyatt	1923-1957	1141	157	232	39405	40.04
DCS Compton	1936-1964	839	88	300	38942	51.85
GE Tyldesley	1909-1936	961	106	256*	38874	45.46
JT Tyldesley	1895-1923	993	62	295*	37896	40.70
JW Hearne	1909-1936	1025	116	285*	37252	40.98
LEG Ames	1926-1951	951	95	295	37248	43.51
D Kenyon	1946-1967	1159	59	259	37002	33.63
WJ Edrich	1934-1958	964	92	267*	36965	42.39
DL Amiss	1960-1983	954	102	262*	36879	43.28
JM Parks	1949-1976	1227	172	205*	36673	34.76
D Denton	1894-1920	1161	70	221	36440	33.40
GH Hirst	1891-1929	1214	151	341	36272	34.12
A Jones	1957-1983	1168	72	204*	36049	32.89
WG Quaife	1894-1928	1203	185	255*	36016	35.37
RE Marshall	1945-1972	1053	59	228*	35725	35.94
G Gunn	1902-1932	1061	82	220	35208	35.96
DB Close	1949-1983	1220	170	198	34911	33.24
JG Langridge	1928-1955	984	66	250*	34380	37.45
GM Turner	1964-1982	792	101	311*	34346	49.70
C Washbrook	1933-1964	906	107	251*	34101	42.67
KWR Fletcher	1962-1983	1025	146	228*	33957	38.63
M Leyland	1920-1948	932	101	263	33659	40.50
HTW Hardinge	1902-1933	1021	103	263*	33519	36.51
R Abel	1881-1904	1007	73	357*	33124	35.46
Zaheer Abbas	1965-1983	682	80	274	32307	53.66

FIRST-CLASS CRICKET RECORDS

CA Milton	1948-1974	1078	125	170	32150	33.73
JDB Robertson	1937-1959	897	46	331*	31914	37.50
J Hardstaff jr	1930-1955	812	94	266	31847	44.35
James Langridge	1924-1953	1058	157	167	31716	35.20
KF Barrington	1953-1968	831	136	256	31714	45.63
Mushtaq Mohd	1956-1983	840	104	303*	31044	42.17
CB Fry	1892-1921	658	43	258*	30886	50.22
D Brookes	1934-1959	925	70	257	30874	36.10
P Holmes	1913-1935	810	84	315*	30574	42.11
RT Simpson	1944-1963	852	55	259	30546	38.32
GL Berry	1924-1951	1056	57	232	30225	30.25
KG Suttle	1949-1971	1064	92	204*	30225	31.09

LEADING CENTURY-MAKERS (100 HUNDREDS)

	Career	100s	Innings
JB Hobbs	1905-1934	197	1315
EH Hendren	1907-1938	170	1300
WR Hammond	1920-1951	167	1005
CP Mead	1905-1936	153	1340
H Sutcliffe	1919-1945	149	1088
FE Woolley	1906-1938	145	1532
G Boycott	1962-1983	139	925
L Hutton	1934-1960	129	814
WG Grace	1865-1908	124	1478
DCS Compton	1936-1964	123	839
TW Graveney	1948-1971	122	1223
DG Bradman	1927-1948	117	338
A Sandham	1911-1937	107	1000
MC Cowdrey	1950-1976	107	1130
Zaheer Abbas	1965-1983	105	682
TW Hayward	1893-1914	104	1138
JH Edrich	1956-1978	103	979
GM Turner	1964-1982	103	792
LEG Ames	1926-1951	102	951
GE Tyldesley	1909-1936	102	961

BOWLING: LEADING AGGREGATES (2,000 WICKETS)

	Career	Runs	Wkts	Avge
W Rhodes	1898-1930	69939	4187	16.70
AP Freeman	1914-1936	69577	3776	18.42
CWL Parker	1903-1935	63817	3278	19.46
JT Hearne	1888-1923	54361	3061	17.75
TWJ Goddard	1922-1952	59116	2979	19.84
AS Kennedy	1907-1936	61044	2874	21.24

FIRST-CLASS CRICKET RECORDS

D Shackleton	1948-1969	53303	2857	18.65
GAR Lock	1946-1970	54710	2844	19.23
FJ Titmus	1949-1982	63313	2830	22.37
WG Grace	1865-1908	50932	2809	18.13
MW Tate	1912-1937	50567	2784	18.16
GH Hirst	1891-1929	51231	2733	18.74
C Blythe	1899-1914	42136	2506	16.81
WE Astill	1906-1939	57783	2431	23.76
JC White	1909-1937	43759	2356	18.57
WE Hollies	1932-1957	48656	2323	20.94
FS Trueman	1949-1969	42154	2304	18.29
JB Statham	1950-1968	36995	2260	16.36
RTD Perks	1930-1955	53770	2233	24.07
DL Underwood	1963-1983	44014	2224	19.79
J Briggs	1879-1900	35390	2221	15.93
DJ Shepherd	1950-1972	47298	2218	21.32
EG Dennett	1903-1926	42571	2147	19.82
T Richardson	1892-1905	38794	2105	18.42
TE Bailey	1945-1967	48170	2082	23.13
R Illingworth	1951-1983	42023	2072	20.28
FE Woolley	1906-1938	41066	2068	19.85
G Geary	1912-1938	41339	2063	20.03
DVP Wright	1932-1957	49305	2056	23.98
JA Newman	1906-1930	51211	2032	25.20
A Shaw	1864-1897	24496	2021	12.12
S Haigh	1895-1913	32091	2012	15.94

WICKET-KEEPING: LEADING AGGREGATES (1,000 DISMISSALS) †

	Career	Dismissals	Ct	St
RW Taylor	1960-1983	1594	1424	170
JT Murray	1952-1975	1527	1270	257
H Strudwick	1902-1927	1491	1239	252
FH Huish	1895-1914	1328	952	376
D Hunter	1889-1909	1327	955	372
B Taylor	1949-1973	1294	1082	212
HR Butt	1890-1912	1262	971	291
APE Knott	1964-1983	1260	1129	131
JH Board	1890-1914	1206	852	354
H Elliott	1920-1947	1206	904	302
JM Parks	1949-1976	1182	1089	93
R Booth	1951-1970	1122	946	176
LEG Ames	1926-1951	1113	698	415
G Duckworth	1923-1947	1090	751	339
HW Stephenson	1948-1964	1084	752	332
JG Binks	1955-1975	1071	895	176
TG Evans	1939-1969	1060	811	249
A Long	1960-1980	1046	922	124

FIRST-CLASS CRICKET RECORDS

GO Dawkes	1937-1961	1042	896	146
RW Tolchard	1965-1983	1037	912	125
WL Cornford	1921-1947	1000	656	344

† Including any catches taken in the field.

FIELDING: LEADING AGGREGATES (500 CATCHES)

	Career	Catches
FE Woolley	1906-1938	1018
WG Grace	1865-1908	866
GAR Lock	1946-1970	830
WR Hammond	1920-1951	819
DB Close	1949-1983	811
JG Langridge	1928-1955	786
EH Hendren	1907-1938	755
CA Milton	1948-1974	755
W Rhodes	1898-1930	707
PM Walker	1956-1972	697
J Tunnicliffe	1891-1907	691
CP Mead	1905-1936	668
MC Cowdrey	1950-1976	638
MJ Stewart	1954-1972	634
James Seymour	1900-1926	622
PJ Sharpe	1956-1976	617
PJ Sainsbury	1954-1976	616
KJ Grieves	1945-1964	610
EG Hayes	1896-1926	609
PGH Fender	1910-1936	599
GRJ Roope	1964-1982	599
ASM Oakman	1947-1968	594
MJK Smith	1951-1975	593
R Abel	1881-1904	585
DC Morgan	1950-1969	573
KWR Fletcher	1962-1983	564
PH Parfitt	1956-1974	564
TW Graveney	1948-1971	550
GH Hirst	1891-1929	549
AO Jones	1892-1914	548
JV Wilson	1946-1963	545
LC Braund	1896-1920	544
WJ Edrich	1934-1958	526
AS Kennedy	1907-1936	523
DS Steele	1963-1983	517
KF Barrington	1953-1968	513
GR Cox	1895-1928	510
DB Carr	1945-1968	501

† Including any catches taken when deputising as wicket-keeper.

FIRST CLASS CRICKET RECORDS

FIRST-CLASS COMPETITIONS

ENGLAND

The County Championship

1890	Surrey	1923	Yorks	1956	Surrey
1891	Surrey	1924	Yorks	1957	Surrey
1892	Surrey	1925	Yorks	1958	Surrey
1893	Yorks	1926	Lancs	1959	Yorks
1894	Surrey	1927	Lancs	1960	Yorks
1895	Surrey	1928	Lancs	1961	Hants
1896	Yorks	1929	Notts	1962	Yorks
1897	Lancs	1930	Lancs	1963	Yorks
1898	Yorks	1931	Yorks	1964	Worcs
1899	Surrey	1932	Yorks	1965	Worcs
1900	Yorks	1933	Yorks	1966	Yorks
1901	Yorks	1934	Lancs	1967	Yorks
1902	Yorks	1935	Yorks	1968	Yorks
1903	Middx	1936	Derbys	1969	Glam
1904	Lancs	1937	Yorks	1970	Kent
1905	Yorks	1938	Yorks	1971	Surrey
1906	Kent	1939	Yorks	1972	Warwicks
1907	Notts	1946	Yorks	1973	Hants
1908	Yorks	1947	Middx	1974	Worcs
1909	Kent	1948	Glam	1975	Leics
1910	Kent	1949	{Middx / Yorks}	1976	Middx
1911	Warwicks			1977	{Middx / Kent}
1912	Yorks	1950	{Lancs / Surrey}		
1913	Kent			1978	Kent
1914	Surrey	1951	Warwicks	1979	Essex
1919	Yorks	1952	Surrey	1980	Middx
1920	Middx	1953	Surrey	1981	Notts
1921	Middx	1954	Surrey	1982	Middx
1922	Yorks	1955	Surrey	1983	Essex

Most outright titles (1890 to date): 29—Yorkshire
Earliest date for winning title: 12 August—Kent in 1910

AUSTRALIA

The Sheffield Shield since 1945

1946-47	Victoria	1955-56	New South Wales
1947-48	Western Australia	1956-57	New South Wales
1948-49	New South Wales	1957-58	New South Wales
1949-50	New South Wales	1958-59	New South Wales
1950-51	Victoria	1959-60	New South Wales
1951-52	New South Wales	1960-61	New South Wales
1952-53	South Australia	1961-62	New South Wales
1953-54	New South Wales	1962-63	Victoria
1954-55	New South Wales	1963-64	South Australia

FIRST CLASS CRICKET RECORDS

1964-65	New South Wales	1974-75	Western Australia
1965-66	New South Wales	1975-76	South Australia
1966-67	Victoria	1976-77	Western Australia
1967-68	Western Australia	1977-78	Western Australia
1968-69	South Australia	1978-79	Victoria
1969-70	Victoria	1979-80	Victoria
1970-71	South Australia	1980-81	Western Australia
1971-72	Western Australia	1981-82	South Australia
1972-73	Western Australia	1982-83	New South Wales
1973-74	Victoria		

Titles since 1892:
New South Wales 37, Victoria 24, South Australia 12, Western Australia 8, Queensland and Tasmania 0.

SOUTH AFRICA

The Currie Cup since 1945

1946-47	Natal	1968-69	Transvaal
1947-48	Natal	1969-70	{ Transvaal / Western Province }
1950-51	Transvaal		
1951-52	Natal	1970-71	Transvaal
1952-53	Western Province	1971-72	Transvaal
1954-55	Natal	1972-73	Transvaal
1955-56	Western Province	1973-74	Natal
1958-59	Transvaal	1974-75	Western Province
1959-60	Natal	1975-76	Natal
1960-61	Natal	1976-77	Natal
1962-63	Natal	1977-78	Western Province
1963-64	Natal	1978-79	Transvaal
1965-66	{ Natal / Transvaal }	1979-80	Transvaal
		1980-81	Natal
1966-67	Natal	1981-82	Western Province
1967-68	Natal	1982-83	Transvaal

Titles since 1889:
Transvaal 20, Natal 18, Western Province 12, Kimberley (now Griqualand West) 1.
Shared titles: Transvaal 4, Natal 3, Western Province 2.

Section B Winners

1951-52	Orange Free State	1967-68	Rhodesia
1952-53	Transvaal	1968-69	Western Province
1954-55	Eastern Province	1969-70	Transvaal B
1955-56	Rhodesia	1970-71	Rhodesia
1958-59	Border	1971-72	Northern Transvaal
1959-60	{ Eastern Province / Transvaal B }	1972-73	Transvaal B
		1973-74	Natal B
1962-63	Transvaal B	1974-75	Transvaal B
1963-64	Rhodesia	1975-76	Orange Free State
1965-66	North-Eastern Transvaal	1976-77	Transvaal B
1966-67	North-Eastern Transvaal	1977-78	Northern Transvaal

FIRST CLASS CRICKET RECORDS

1978-79	Northern Transvaal	1981-82	Boland
1979-80	Natal B	1982-83	Western Province B
1980-81	Western Province B		

WEST INDIES
The Shell Shield

1965-66	Barbados	1975-76	Barbados / Trinidad
1966-67	Barbados		
1968-69	Jamaica	1976-77	Barbados
1969-70	Trinidad	1977-78	Barbados
1970-71	Trinidad	1978-79	Barbados
1971-72	Barbados	1979-80	Barbados
1972-73	Guyana	1980-81	Combined Islands
1973-74	Barbados	1981-82	Barbados
1974-75	Guyana	1982-83	Guyana

Titles: Barbados 9, Guyana 3, Trinidad 2, Combined Islands and Jamaica 1.
Shared titles: Barbados and Trinidad 1.

NEW ZEALAND
The Plunket Shield

1945-46	Canterbury	1960-61	Wellington
1946-47	Auckland	1961-62	Wellington
1947-48	Otago	1962-63	Northern Districts
1948-49	Canterbury	1963-64	Auckland
1949-50	Wellington	1964-65	Canterbury
1950-51	Otago	1965-66	Wellington
1951-52	Canterbury	1966-67	Central Districts
1952-53	Otago	1967-68	Central Districts
1953-54	Central Districts	1968-69	Auckland
1954-55	Wellington	1969-70	Otago
1955-56	Canterbury	1970-71	Central Districts
1956-57	Wellington	1971-72	Otago
1957-58	Otago	1972-73	Wellington
1958-59	Auckland	1973-74	Wellington
1959-60	Canterbury	1974-75	Otago

Shell Trophy

1975-76	Canterbury	1979-80	Northern Districts
1976-77	Otago	1980-81	Auckland
1977-78	Auckland	1981-82	Wellington
1978-79	Otago	1982-83	Wellington

INDIA
Ranji Trophy

1946-47	Baroda	1947-48	Holkar

FIRST CLASS CRICKET RECORDS

1948-49	Bombay	1959-73	Bombay
1949-50	Baroda	1973-74	Karnataka
1950-51	Holkar	1974-75	Bombay
1951-52	Bombay	1975-76	Bombay
1952-53	Holkar	1976-77	Bombay
1953-54	Bombay	1977-78	Karnataka
1954-55	Madras	1978-79	Delhi
1955-56	Bombay	1979-80	Delhi
1956-57	Bombay	1980-81	Bombay
1957-58	Baroda	1981-82	Delhi
1958-59	Bombay	1982-83	Karnataka

† World record for any national championship of 15 consecutive wins. Bombay lost to Karnataka on the first innings in the 1973-74 semi-finals.

Titles since 1934: Bombay 49, Baroda, Holkar 4, Delhi, Karnataka (Mysore) 3, Maharashtra 2, Bengal, Hyderabad, Tamil Nadu (Madras), Nawanagar, Western India States 1.

The Duleep Trophy

1961-62	West Zone	1972-73	West Zone
1962-63	West Zone	1973-74	North Zone
1963-64	South and West Zones shared trophy	1974-75	South Zone
		1975-76	South Zone
1964-65	West Zone	1976-77	West Zone
1965-66	South Zone	1977-78	West Zone
1966-67	South Zone	1978-79	North Zone
1967-68	South Zone	1979-80	North Zone
1968-69	West Zone	1980-81	West Zone
1969-70	West Zone	1981-82	West Zone
1970-71	South Zone	1982-83	North Zone
1971-72	Central Zone		

PAKISTAN

The Quaid-E-Azam Trophy

1953-54	Bahawalpur	1970-71	Karachi Blues
1954-55	Karachi	1972-73	Railways
1956-57	Punjab	1973-74	Railways
1957-58	Bahawalpur	1974-75	Punjab
1958-59	Karachi	1975-76	National Bank
1959-60	Karachi	1976-77	United Bank
1961-62	Karachi Blues	1977-78	Habib Bank
1962-63	Karachi	1978-79	National Bank
1963-64	Karachi Blues	1979-80	PIA
1964-65	Karachi Blues	1980-81	United Bank
1966-67	Karachi	1981-82	National Bank
1968-69	Lahore	1982-83	United Bank
1969-70	PIA		

TEST GROUNDS

Until the middle 1920s Test cricket had been played on only 15 grounds. With the rise to Test status of West Indies, New Zealand, India, Pakistan and eventually in 1981 Sri Lanka, this has grown to over 50. It is still growing, mainly on the sub-continent of India, as industry and populations expand and the proliferation of Test matches makes it sensible to spread the interest around. South African grounds are in abeyance as Test venues but only two cities seem to have lost their Test cricket—Sheffield, where one Test match was played in 1902, and Dacca, once capital of East Pakistan but now of Bangladesh.

AUSTRALIA

MELBOURNE CRICKET GROUND (MCG)

The first Test match of all was played in Melbourne and more than 100 years later the Melbourne Cricket Ground is still the largest in the world. Its already huge capacity was increased (and its surface levelled) to accommodate the Olympic Games of 1956 and now crowds of 120,000 fill it for the Australian Rules football grand finals. For cricket the biggest is the 90,800 which watched the Saturday's play in the final Test between Australia and West indies in 1960-61.

The Melbourne Cricket Club moved its ground to its present site in 1853. The playing area is still vast even by Australian standards but in recent years the square has often been unsatisfactory, possibly because the high stands keep out light and wind. Excavation has brought better pitches in the 1980s. It is a weakness that despite the groves of gum trees which surround the ground and provide an area for car parking facilities, there is no second ground for nets and practice. But it is a magnificent arena within walking distance of the centre of a city of immense sporting enthusiasm.

SYDNEY CRICKET GROUND (SCG)

The Sydney Cricket Ground accommodates barely half the number of the MCG but has a special cricket atmosphere akin to that of Lord's. It has lost some of its old character with two new stands and six huge pylons erected in 1978 for floodlighting, but it usually provides good pitches, despite the football played over it in the winter. The Hill, a large grassy bank across the ground from the pavilion, used to be famous for the wit of the spectators who occupied it and is a special feature of the ground even if the wit is in shorter supply in the unruly 1980s. Within a short bus ride of the city centre, the SCG is administered by a Trust made up of political appointees but including a few former New South Wales cricketers. There is a spacious No2 ground behind the pavilion, Bradman and Noble stands, which provides net and practice facilities.

ADELAIDE OVAL

The Adelaide Oval is a true oval, considerably longer than it is broad. A straight drive will run over 100 yards to the boundary, a cut barely 75. It is one of the most charming big grounds in the world—it holds 40,000—and whether the spectator faces St Peter's Cathedral at the north end, the skyline of the city half a mile away across the River Torrens to the south, the distant Mount Lofty range to the east or the trees beyond the pavilion and members enclosure, it remains a wonderfully pleasant place to watch cricket. There are usually splendid batting pitches at the Adelaide Oval where the first Test was played in 1884, only two years after Sydney's first. But, though a Test is played there in every full series, Adelaide with its smaller population has never aspired to the two matches usually allotted in alternate series to Melbourne or Sydney.

WOOLLOONGABBA, BRISBANE

Test cricket in Brisbane began in 1928 at the Exhibition Ground but this was only used twice and from 1931 the Woolloongabba ground known as the 'Gabba' has been the setting in a suburb of corrugated iron roofs. Despite its sub-tropical trees, it is not the most picturesque ground, but pays its way through its regular use for greyhound racing. It earned undying fame by staging, in December 1960, the historic tied Test between Australia and West Indies. For many years the Gabba had the unique distinction of having the Lord Mayor of the city as its groundsman or curator. Alderman Clem Jones had to cope with many crises, for Brisbane is sometimes afflicted by violent thunderstorms which are capable of penetrating the stoutest of pitch covers.

WESTERN AUSTRALIA CRICKET ASSOCIATION GROUND (WACA), PERTH

If it seems strange that the first Test at Perth was not staged there until 1970, it has to be remembered that it was only in 1956-57 that Western Australia were admitted to full membership of the Sheffield Shield competition, as air travel improved. The Western Australia Cricket Association ground, known as the 'Waca' (pronounced Wacker), is a pleasant relatively open ground seldom required to accommodate more than 15,000. It used to have a reputation for providing the fastest and truest pitches in the world but that was not always so in the 1970s. It has one characteristic of its own. On the hottest days, a cool southerly breeze, the 'Fremantle Doctor', often starts to blow across the broad estuary of the nearby Swan River at about four o'clock in the afternoon, making unwary spectators wish that they had brought a pullover and providing a subtle aid to the spin bowler who flights the ball.

TEST GROUNDS

ENGLAND

THE OVAL, KENNINGTON

As the scene of the first two Test matches played in England, the Oval, in Kennington within sight of Big Ben, has a special historical significance. The first Test in September 1880 was organised by the then Surrey secretary, CW Alcock, and was watched over its three days by 44,000. Less than 40 years earlier the ground had been a market garden and its development, not only for cricket but for other events, was not smooth. Surrey were not happy with it as a cricket ground and their landlords, the Duchy of Cornwall, considered selling it for building purposes. This last move was stopped by Prince Albert and a new lease between club and landlords was negotiated. Their association continues today, though the neighbourhood has changed from one of parkland to one of gasholders, factories and flats typical of the area just south of the Thames.

The playing-area, the biggest of any first-class ground in England, was used for football at various periods—the FA Cup final was played there at one time and some early rugby internationals—and in 1939 was prepared as a prisoner-of-war camp. It was not used as such but the ground deteriorated and much hard work was needed to restore it for the 1946 season.

Briefly then the home ground of Jack Hobbs was again a joyous one for batsmen with a fast if rough outfield but in the 1950s, when Surrey won the county championship seven times running, the pitches were less easy, the outfield lush, the great Surrey bowlers, Bedser and Loader, Laker and Lock, destroyed many opponents and it required a batsman of the class of Peter May to score consistently there. Since the Second World War seats have been installed where there were once earth mounds and the ground capacity has been reduced to under 20,000.

LORD'S, ST JOHNS WOOD

When Lord's staged its first Test in 1884, the ground, the third found by Thomas Lord for members of the Marylebone Cricket Club, had already been open for 70 years. MCC had bought the freehold—belatedly—in 1866 for £18,000. Though rebuilding has been and will continue to be necessary, the most famous cricket ground in the world has retained its sense of grandeur and remains a superb place to watch cricket. When some 6,000 spectators are sitting on the grass, it will now hold about 26,000. Unexpectedly for so important a ground there is a slope of some eight feet from the Grand Stand with its Father Time weathervane, down to the Tavern boundary. The old Tavern was demolished in the 1960s and a new one built about 70 yards away beside the Grace Gates, now an impressive main entrance.

The pavilion, built in 1890, has been much rebuilt inside to accommodate offices but the Long Room remains a stately room and the building itself stands with dignity over a ground on which much cricket history has been made. Its amenities include a real tennis court, squash courts, a second ground at the Nursery end on which now stands a fine cricket indoor school built in the 1970s.

The ground is the headquarters not only of MCC but of Middlesex, who play most of their home matches there. The Test and County Cricket Board and the National Cricket Association have offices there and, as the secretariat of MCC is also that of the International Cricket Conference, many decisions affecting the whole cricket world are taken in the Committee Room where the annual ICC meeting takes place. Concern about the wear and tear on a square little over half as broad as that of The Oval has led to a severe reduction in fixtures since the Second World War. Many school and services matches are now played elsewhere, though Oxford and Cambridge, who first played at Lord's in 1827, still meet there, as do Eton and Harrow who met on the original Lord's ground in 1805.

OLD TRAFFORD, MANCHESTER

It is not often realised that Old Trafford, where the Manchester Cricket Club built its ground in the 1850s, preceded Lord's as a Test match ground by 11 days in July 1884. With spectators sitting on the grass round a large playing area, it can still accommodate nearly 25,000 and has an adjoining ground for use as a car park as well as for practice facilities.

Conveniently situated beside Warwick Road station in the southern suburbs of Manchester, it has always had a superb outfield, but its pitches have varied between the flawless one on which Bobby Simpson made 311 out of Australia's 656 for eight declared in 1964 (England replied with 611) to the one on which in the rain-affected 1956 Test, Jim Laker took his surely unbeatable 19 wickets. It was the scene of a famous match in 1902 when Victor Trumper made a 100 before lunch on the first day and Australia won by three runs.

TRENT BRIDGE, NOTTINGHAM

Trent Bridge, across the River Trent from the centre of Nottingham, is a ground with a great tradition of cricket, arising from the days when William Clarke, having married in 1837 the widow who owned the Trent Bridge Inn, developed the field attached to the Inn as a cricket ground. His wandering All England XI became the most famous of the day and Nottinghamshire the home of many famous cricketers. An elm into which one of them, George Parr, used to hit the ball became famous as 'George Parr's tree' and survived until 1976 when it was blown down in a gale.

TEST GROUNDS

The six acres provide a beautifully smooth outfield and the ground retains much of its character. Its stands are mostly of another era, the pavilion has a long room in the old style. The pitches have varied through the years. In the 1930s Larwood and Voce were a formidable combination but in the 1950s the pitches had become 'featherbeds', frustrating bowlers of all types. That has been rectified and they now strike a reasonable balance between bat and ball.

HEADINGLEY, LEEDS

Headingley, in the high northern suburbs of Leeds, is the property not of Yorkshire but of the Leeds Cricket, Football and Athletic Club. At the lower end of the ground, which has a pronounced slope, not as at Lord's from side to side but from end to end, is the foremost Rugby League ground in the country.

Yorkshire have a long lease on the cricket ground which has a new pavilion parallel to the pitch, housing the club offices. Helped by its slope the ground has one of the fastest outfields among Test arenas. It was here that Sir Donald Bradman made over 300 in a day in the 1930 Test and where in 1948 he led Australia to score 404 for three in the last innings, still the highest Test-winning fourth innings in England. In six innings at Headingley he made 963 runs, averaging 192.60. It was not until 1899 that a Test match was played at Headingley but in deference to the traditional Yorkshire zest for cricket, it is allotted a Test match every year.

EDGBASTON, BIRMINGHAM

As a Test ground Edgbaston has had a chequered record. Though conveniently situated in a residential suburb near the centre of Birmingham, it has never had the atmosphere of the other Midlands Test ground, Trent Bridge. The Warwickshire County Cricket Club built the ground in the 1880s and staged their first Test in 1902. It was marred by rain, Australia were bowled out for 36. The next three Tests played there, in 1909 against Australia and in 1924 and 1929 against South Africa, were not a success either. Edgbaston was dropped after 1929 as a Test ground.

However, after the Second World War, Warwickshire, helped by an enterprising Supporters' Club which ran a lucrative football pool, earned a well deserved reputation for enterprise and efficient administration. The ground, indeed the whole property, was rebuilt except for the pavilion which, though rebuilt inside, retains its old exterior.

It was thus on a new and well equipped ground that after a lapse of 28 years England played another Test match there in 1957, a famous match in which Peter May and Colin Cowdrey with their stand of 411 won the initiative, which England were to hold throughout the series, though the Edgbaston match was drawn. Edgbaston's pitches have lacked pace through the years but its facilities in most respects are second to none.

TEST GROUNDS

SOUTH AFRICA

ST GEORGE'S, PORT ELIZABETH
Third into the Test-playing field, South Africa first played England in March 1889 at Port Elizabeth. The St George's ground, on the escarpment above the main business section of the city and the port, is the oldest in the country—the club was formed in 1843, only 23 years after the British settlers landed in Algoa Bay. It is a friendly ground in an area of large houses and clubs with a big stand the length of one side housing pavilion and offices. The pitches are not the best in South Africa, perhaps because of the extremes of drought and deluge sometimes experienced in the eastern Cape.

NEWLANDS, CAPE TOWN
The Newlands ground in Cape Town would be most people's choice among the most beautiful Test grounds in the world. The spectator can sit in the shade of the magnificent oaks on one side and look across at the marvellous backcloth of Table Mountain. Home of the Western Province Cricket Club, Newlands holds barely 14,000 but this can be stretched to about 20,000 by extra stands. The pitches have sometimes lacked bounce but if ever there were a place where the surroundings take precedence over the cricket, this would be it. The England team led by C Aubrey Smith in 1888-89 played two matches against South Africa's best side and these have come to be recognised as the first Tests in the country. The second was at Newlands where England's left-arm spin bowler, Johnny Briggs, took 15 wickets for 28, hitting the stumps 14 times and having one batsman lbw.

WANDERERS GROUND, JOHANNESBURG
Johannesburg has had three Test grounds. Its first was the old Wanderers Club ground in the centre of the city where a Test match was played in 1896, only 10 years after the discovery of gold started the transformation of a piece of bare veld into a thriving city. The ground was used for 22 Tests up to the Second World War after which it was taken over by the railway system. The Wanderers Club used the money from the disposal of their valuable real estate to build a new ground in the northern outskirts of the city.

Meanwhile Test matches, six of them between 1948 and 1954, were played on the rugby ground at Ellis Park.

The new Wanderers ground, with its one big covered cantilever-type stand behind the bowler's arm and the rest high open terraced seating, is a fine modern ground. It was ready for a Test match when England arrived in 1956-57—usually two are played there in each series—and it was the scene in December 1966 of a remarkable match in which Australia, having bowled out South Africa for 199 and

TEST GROUNDS

taken first innings lead with only one wicket down, eventually lost by 233 runs. It was their first Test defeat in South Africa.

KINGSMEAD, DURBAN

Kingsmead in Durban is the second ground in the city used for Test cricket. The first, called Lord's, was the scene of four Tests between 1909-10 and the first Australian visit late in 1921. Kingsmead, half a mile inland and marginally below sea level, has its main stand and pavilion square to the pitch. Its outfield of kikuyu grass can be one of the slowest, or, if shaved, one of the fastest in the world. The pitches have varied greatly, helped by the humid climate.

Kingsmead's most famous match was the Timeless Test of March 1939 when England, needing 696 to win, had to give up after 10 days to catch their ship home, with their score 654 for five.

WEST INDIES

Four of West Indies' Test grounds were used in their first home Test series against England early in 1930. Not until 1981 when England played in Antigua was a fifth added, the practice having been to play two in Trinidad where the crowds are greatest. West Indian crowds, however, are fickle and there have been ill-attended matches, even in Port of Spain, when the series has already been lost or, as in 1981, the selectors have omitted a popular Trinidadian, in that case Deryck Murray.

QUEEN'S PARK OVAL, PORT-OF-SPAIN, TRINIDAD

Only half a mile from the Savannah, the parkland heart of the city, the Queen's Park Oval provides a broad and beautiful view of the Northern Range of hills with their tropical vegetation. It is one of the world's most striking grounds, though the behaviour of mortals has not always matched the graciousness of nature and matches have been marred by riots. The ground had matting pitches long after others in the Caribbean had turned to grass. It was only in the 1950s that turf pitches were introduced—with overall success.

KENSINGTON OVAL, BRIDGETOWN, BARBADOS

The influence on cricket history of Barbados, roughly the size of the Isle of Wight, with its apparently bottomless well of talent, has long been a sporting marvel but the Kensington Oval in Bridgetown holds no more than 10,000 and is notable for the enthusiasm of those who turn up rather than for its charm. It reflects the modest economy of the island rather than its cricket talent. The pitches rarely lack pace, though recently they have not always been as true as when Hanif Mohammad made 337 for Pakistan here in 1957-58, at 999 minutes the longest Test innings; or when the three Ws, Worrell, Weekes

TEST GROUNDS

and Walcott made thousands of runs there during and after the Second World War.

SABINA PARK, KINGSTON, JAMAICA

Sabina Park has always been the Test ground in Jamaica, though its straight boundary, barely 60 yards, is one of the shortest on any first-class ground. Though it was here that the great George Headley played most of his cricket and that Gary Sobers set the Test record score of 365 not out against Pakistan in 1957-58, this has also been a ground on which fast bowlers prospered. Trevor Bailey's seven for 34 after West Indies had chosen to bat paved the way for England's victory in the final Test of 1953-54 and for West Indies' first defeat at Sabina Park. As in Trinidad there is an attractive, if more distant, view of mountains but the ground, much of it reconstructed in the 1980s, is practical and accessible rather than beautiful.

BOURDA, GEORGETOWN, GUYANA

West Indies' first victory over England came in the first Test played in Georgetown, in what is now Guyana, but the last scheduled meeting between the two countries there was a sad affair. Incessant rain had washed out the match against Guyana in 1981 and was threatening the Test match when the Guyanan government withdrew Robin Jackman's visitor's permit because he had been to South Africa recently and the England team left the country. In better times the Bourda ground, like most of Georgetown below sea level, is one on which batsmen prosper but although many of West Indies' finest players of recent years—Lloyd, Kanhai, Kallicharran, Butcher, Lance Gibbs, and Croft among them—have come from Guyana, riots have marred some of the cricket there.

RECREATION GROUND, ST JOHN'S, ANTIGUA

With Antigua's growing attraction as a tourist island and its production in the 1970s of both a great batsman, Vivian Richards, and a great fast bowler, Andy Roberts, its arrival as a Test centre was inevitable. In 1981 England's first Test there was played on one of the best pitches encountered on the tour. The ground, across the road from Government House in the capital, St John's, is most notable for having convicts from the local gaol as its willing ground staff.

NEW ZEALAND

New Zealand played their first Test match at Christchurch in January 1930 and, apart from one match against Pakistan at Napier in 1979, have played all their Tests at Christchurch, Auckland, Wellington or Dunedin. Of these four, only Wellington is not also an international rugby ground, so the groundsmen have no easy task in preparing a cricket square, especially in the first half of the season.

TEST GROUNDS

LANCASTER PARK, CHRISTCHURCH
Lancaster Park in Christchurch is a ground of some character with a fine view of the Cashmere Hills. New Zealand have had some moments there on indifferent pitches, as when England bowled them out for 65 on the first day in 1970-71, but it was at Christchurch that in 1974 they beat Australia for the first time and the memory of that is sweet.

BASIN RESERVE, WELLINGTON
A unique history clings to this ground, for it was originally a lake which, it was intended, should be made into an inner harbour. An earthquake in 1853 turned the lake into a swamp and the cricketers, who had lost their own ground, asked if they could make one out of the swamp. They were given permission and by 1868 were playing on it. Some low scores have been made on it, notably the 42 and 54 by New Zealand in their first Test against Australia in 1946, but Jackie McGlew's 255 in 1953 was the highest until then by a South African. Often it is the gale which upsets the batsman, coming as it can do from opposite directions on successive days. It was at full blast when England were bowled out for 64 in 1978 and lost their first Test to New Zealand.

EDEN PARK, AUCKLAND
Eden Park in Auckland can hold up to 40,000 and the importance to New Zealand cricket finances of fine weather and a Test there is immense. The square is laid diagonally across the rugby field but the climate is almost sub-tropical, recovery is quicker than in the south and many good batting pitches are obtained here. The ground, set in a hilly suburb of Auckland, is well appointed with fine new offices for both rugby and cricket. It was here in 1956 that, after 26 years of trying, New Zealand won their first Test beating West Indies by 190 runs.

CARISBROOK, DUNEDIN
Carisbrook, another famous rugby ground, produces despite its winter usage one of the most perfectly grassed outfields in the world. Otago, the home province, has produced some great players, notably Bert Sutcliffe and Glenn Turner, and though the pitches are similar to those in Scotland, with which Dunedin has so much in common climatically and otherwise, Carisbrook produces some good cricket.

McLEAN PARK, NAPIER
Napier, on the east coast of the North Island, staged its one Test when Basin Reserve at Wellington was undergoing reconstruction. The pitch at McLean Park, an unknown quantity for a five-day match, was a good one which, even without interruptions from rain, made a draw almost certain.

TEST GROUNDS

INDIA

India has had more Test centres than any other country, 11 up to 1984.

WANKHEDE STADIUM, BOMBAY

Bombay was the first city to stage a Test match, the only one on the Gymkhana ground, for from 1948 the venue was the Brabourne Stadium, home of the Cricket Club of India. Financial disputes between the CCI and the Bombay Cricket Association led to the building of an even larger ground only a few blocks away. The Wankhede Stadium was first used in 1975 and like other modern grounds in India is a concrete bowl holding over 40,000.

EDEN GARDENS, CALCUTTA

Eden Gardens in Calcutta is India's oldest Test ground, first used for Test cricket in 1934. Standing between the broad maidan and the Hooghly river, it is also one of the oldest club grounds in the world, founded by the Calcutta Cricket Club. Always large, even though its stands were partly improvised, it became after rebuilding in the 1970s the second largest cricket ground in the world after Melbourne, a huge concrete arena accommodating 70,000. It is also probably the best attended, for even in 1977 when on the fifth morning India faced certain defeat within about an hour's play, it was still full. The pitches, when not shaved, are among the grassiest in India and conditions favour the faster bowlers as they do on few other grounds on the sub-continent.

M A CHIDAMBARAM, MADRAS

Madras, the third of the original Test centres used for the visit of D R Jardine's England team in 1933-34, is unique in having returned to the ground which was its original setting. Up to 1952-53 Chepauk, an attractive almost English-type ground on which many fine English cricketers played in the days of the Raj, staged 13 Tests, but while the Board waited for the lease held by the Madras CC to run out, they were switched to the Corporation ground. By 1966-67, however, Test cricket was back at Chepauk, now a huge concrete bowl totally unrecognisable to former players and renamed the M A Chidambaram after the great administrator and benefactor of modern Indian cricket. After its rebuilding it soon earned a reputation for crumbling pitches on which India's brilliant spinners of the day thrived but England, to their surprise, found themselves playing there in 1976-77 on one of the fastest Test pitches many could remember and won with their fast bowlers.

FEROZSHAH KOTLA, DELHI

Delhi did not stage a Test match until 1949, as the ground,

TEST GROUNDS

Ferozshah Kotla, situated between Old and New Delhi, was dusty and ill-equipped. When the north wind blows off the Himalayas it can be a cold place to watch cricket, if one is not in the sun. The pitches are usually good and it is the amount which the ball swung which won England an unexpectedly easy victory in 1976-77.

GREEN PARK, KANPUR

Kanpur was allotted its first Test on the Green Park ground in 1950-51. Green is a misnomer at most times of year. Its early Tests were played on matting and when the move to grass, or more properly mud, took place, Australia were beaten in 1959-60 on a poor pitch which took spin extravagantly. However, that proved untypical of subsequent pitches which have been of baked clay too slow to inspire an absorbing cricket match.

OTHER TEST GROUNDS

A Test match, which Pakistan won by an innings, was played in Lucknow in 1952. Nagpur had grown enough to warrant a Test against New Zealand in 1969-70 and another late in 1983 when Jullundur in the far north also staged one in a series against India. Hyderabad, in the Deccan, was the scene of two drawn Tests against New Zealand in 1955-56 and four years later.

However, in the 1970s, Bangalore in Southern India, one of the country's most pleasant cities, built a new large concrete stadium in the old cantonment area of the British Army. The first Test in the Karnataka CA Stadium was played against West Indies in 1974-75 and its popularity, not least among players, suggests that it will in future be given a Test in most series. Late in 1983 a first Test was staged in the big north-western city of Ahmedabad, when West Indies played there.

PAKISTAN

GADDAFI STADIUM, LAHORE

Pakistan in their short history have played Test cricket in eight cities (including the lost Dacca), though only Lahore and Karachi have large modern grounds. The Gaddafi Stadium in Lahore, a spacious ground on the outskirts of the city, housed its first Test when Australia won there in 1959-60, before which three Tests had been played at Lawrence Gardens. The pitch can have more life than most in Pakistan but this is a relative appraisal, for in their three visits in 10 years from 1968-69 England drew all nine Tests. More than one was interrupted by riots born of either political unrest or of excessive enthusiasm and police reaction to it.

NATIONAL STADIUM, KARACHI

The National Stadium in Karachi, ten miles from the city

centre, is a similar large concrete arena which turned from matting to turf in the 1960s, though baked mud is a more accurate description in an area of meagre rainfall. A slow pitch of low bounce tends to become slower. As in Lahore, Test matches have been plagued by rioting, once in 1969 causing an abandonment on the third morning when England had made 502 for seven.

NIAZ STADIUM, HYDERABAD

Hyderabad (Sind), 100 miles across the desert from Karachi, became a Test centre when England played there in 1972-73. It is as dry as Karachi but the Niaz Stadium is more in the old style of ground and has produced some interesting cricket on pitches which take spin, albeit seldom quickly enough to produce a definite result.

IQBAL STADIUM, FAISALABAD

Faisalabad, formerly Lyallpur, a textile centre, did not have a Test match until England's visit in 1977-78 but the facilities of the Iqbal Stadium have been greatly improved, it can hold over 20,000 and usually provides one of the best batting pitches in the world. As the standard of Pakistan's all-round cricket rises, efforts continue in an unhelpful climate to produce pitches which will provide better cricket and in September and October 1981 a slightly below strength Australian side lost all three Tests at Karachi, Faisalabad and Lahore.

OTHER TEST GROUNDS

Of the grounds used for Tests only once, Dring Stadium in Bahawalpur is a pleasant tree-ringed ground relying on temporary stands to accommodate a big crowd as saw India play there in 1955. Peshawar, near the foot of the Khyber Pass, had its only Test in the same series. The Gymkhana ground is in an area recalling the days of the Raj and appears in record books as the ground where Mike Brearley made 312 not out in a day for the MCC under-25 team against North Zone in 1966-67. In 1965 Pakistan played New Zealand at Rawalpindi on a pleasant ground, centrally placed, and more resembling a local army ground than a modern Test arena.

SRI LANKA

One of the assurances given by Sri Lanka in applying for Test status was that they would provide a sizeable, well equipped modern ground and this was ready in Colombo when after a good match at the Saravanamuttu Oval, capacity 25,000 England won Sri Lanka's first Test in March 1982. However, when Australia called a year later on the way to England for the Prudential World Cup, they played their one Test in more picturesque surroundings at Kandy, several thousand feet up in the interior of the island.

CAPTAINCY AND ITS SIGNIFICANCE

Captaincy of a cricket team almost certainly involves wider responsibility and more decision-taking than leadership in any other sport. Cricket usually takes longer to play than other team games. Thus the captain not only has to maintain harmony and bring the best out of his players on the field but also on and off the field during a tour which may last weeks or months.

The captain has to name his side before the toss takes place and he should have made up his mind already as to what to do if he wins it, which means that he must already have inspected the pitch, probably with his senior players.

The ideal pitch is one which starts fast and true, does not lose its pace and over the second half of the match gives the bowlers, especially the spin bowlers, more help. This ideal will seldom be attained, for the preparation of pitches is influenced by many things—the weather, the type of soil, the type of covering used and the experience and efficiency of the groundsman. Sometimes the subsoil has become so compacted by rolling over the years that it forms a sort of cushion and no amount of good groundsmanship can produce a fast pitch of adequate bounce without digging up the square and relaying it.

Thus the captain has to assess whether the pitch will last or whether it will be at its freshest on the first day and will justify putting the other side in. The old maxim was 'Think about putting the other side in—then bat'. Nowadays there is an increased tendency to choose to field first, partly perhaps because fast bowling now usually has a bigger influence on a match than spin, which means that favourable conditions for bowling in the first innings when the pitch is lively are more desirable than in the fourth innings when the pitch may or may not accommodate bowlers.

The practice of putting the other side in has been further encouraged by its success in one-day cricket, though different conditions apply there. It will be rare for a one-day pitch to deteriorate, so nothing much is lost in that respect by batting second. Moreover, bowling may be easier on a hazy morning, perhaps while a little damp is left in the pitch, just enough perhaps to slow the batting side up if not to upset them.

There are certainly occasions when winning the toss decides the match. Sometimes the opposite may be the case. The pitch may be dry, not too well bound by grass and may be likely to break up. In that case the match may be as good as won in the first half-day by the side batting first.

Groundsmen in England are now under instructions from the Test and County Cricket Board to try to ensure that the pitches in three-day county championship matches start dry.

This, it is hoped, will help the surface of them to deteriorate enough during the second half of the match, for the balance between bat and ball to work out evenly and for all types of bowlers to be used.

But this is not an instruction with which it is always easy to comply. Watering plays a vital part in the preparation of any pitch and the groundsman has to judge when to do his last watering and how thoroughly. The weather forecast may promise that the eve of the match and the early morning will be hot and cloudless. But the sun may not quite break through and the pitch may not dry out as much as he hopes. If a pitch does start damp, batting is often at its hardest on the first day and becomes steadily easier throughout the match until on the last day the bowlers are ineffective and the batsmen need not get out on a now lifeless pitch unless they do something reckless. Good cricket matches are seldom played on pitches which improve.

All this, the type of pitch and the prevailing weather expected during the duration of the match, comes within the captain's consideration.

The captain must also decide his batting order and consider whether circumstances may arise in which a change in the order may be helpful. If so, the players concerned need to be warned.

If his side is in the field, he will be constantly concerned with directing his bowlers, changing them if necessary and arranging his field to cause the maximum inconvenience to the batsman. It will help if he knows already the strengths and weaknesses of the opposing batsmen. If he does not know them, he will keep a close look-out for them, perhaps consulting his wicketkeeper who will be well placed to note any idiosyncrasies.

He will want his fast bowler to bowl downwind. So will his fast bowler! If he has two fast bowlers, he may have them alternating at the downwind end while slower bowlers keep going steadily into the wind—if they are slow spinners, using the wind to make their flight more awkward to the batsman.

There may be times when the captain finds himself frustrated by a long stand, though his bowlers are bowling well. He may then make them change ends in the hope that this will unsettle the batsmen. Experiment, within reason, is a valuable card to hold in one's hand, as is a bowler of different method who by his different pace, flight and trajectory may pose new problems.

THE LAWS OF CRICKET

DEVELOPMENT OF THE LAWS

The Laws of Cricket were first set out in 1744, though rules had probably existed locally in parts of the south of England for most of the century. Various revisions took place until, after the founding of the Marylebone Cricket Club in 1787, the first MCC Code of the Laws was adopted in 1788.

From its formation MCC undertook responsibility for the Laws and by common consent this still rests with the Club in the 1980s, even though the MCC ceased to be the governing body of the game in England in 1969. It is now just a private club—but with two major differences. It maintains responsibility for the Laws of Cricket, and it owns Lord's.

They apply to cricket at all levels but in some instances they have to be flexible to be workable in certain types of competition, for example, in first-class cricket, in limited-over cricket or in competitions at club or school level. In these cases, any departures from the Laws of Cricket should be incorporated in the playing conditions of the particular competition. In friendly matches they should, to forestall misunderstandings, be agreed by both sides.

The major points of the Laws with explanatory notes are set out below.

THE LAWS with explanatory comments

LAW 1 THE PLAYERS
A match is played between two sides of 11 players, one of whom shall be captain. Before the toss for innings the captain shall nominate his players. By agreement a match may be played between sides of more or less than 11 players but not more than 11 may field.

LAW 2 SUBSTITUTES AND RUNNERS
Substitutes shall be allowed to field for any player who, during the match, is incapacitated by illness or injury. The consent of the opposing captain must be obtained for the use of a substitute if any player is prevented from fielding for any other reason.

A player may bat, bowl or field even though a substitute has acted for him, but no substitute may bat or bowl. A fieldsman off the field for more than 15 minutes may not bowl after his return until he has been on the field for at least that length of playing time for which he was absent. (This is intended to deter a bowler from taking a long rest and returning refreshed to his task.)

A runner shall be allowed for a batsman who, during the match, is incapacitated. The runner shall be a member of the batting side and shall, if possible, have already batted in that innings. He shall wear batting gloves and pads if the injured batsman is so equipped.

LAW 3 THE UMPIRES
Before the toss for innings, two umpires shall be appointed. They shall be the sole judges of fair and unfair play, and, with certain minor qualifications, of the fitness of the ground. (If both sides wish to continue, though the umpires consider that conditions are no longer good enough, play continues.)

LAW 4 THE SCORERS
All runs shall be recorded by scorers appointed for the purpose. They shall accept and immediately acknowledge all instructions and signals given to them by the umpires.

LAW 5 THE BALL
The ball shall weigh not less than 155.9g (5½oz), not more than 163g (5¾oz); and shall measure not less than 22.4cm ($8^{13}/_{16}$in), nor more than 22.9cm (9in) in circumference. In a match of three or more days' duration, the fielding captain may demand a new ball after the prescribed number of overs has been bowled with the old one, though this number shall not be less than 75 six-ball overs or 55 eight-ball overs. (Governing bodies throughout the world have the right to decide this number according to the amount of wear the ball receives on their grounds and what they regard as most beneficial to their cricket. The number in countries with hard outfields is usually 75, in England 85, though in first-class matches in England not involving the touring side, it is 100. The Laws also give specifications of smaller balls which may be used for other cricket or for women's and junior cricket.

LAW 6 THE BAT
The bat overall shall not be more than 96.5cm (38in) in length; the blade of the bat shall be made of wood and shall not exceed 10.8cm (4¼in) at the widest part.

LAW 7 THE PITCH
The pitch is the area between the bowling creases. It shall measure 1.52m (5ft) in width. (Sometimes this is called the 'wicket' as in the expression 'sticky wicket' but this is a colloquialism and strictly incorrect.)

LAW 8 THE WICKETS
Two sets of wickets, each 22.86cm (9in) wide, and consisting of three wooden stumps with two wooden bails on top, shall be pitched opposite and parallel to each other at a distance of 20.12m (22yd). The stumps shall be of equal and sufficient size to prevent the ball from passing between them. Their tops shall be 71.1cm (28in) above the ground and shall be

dome-shaped except for the bail grooves. The bails shall be each 11.1cm (4 3/8in) in length and when in position shall not project more than 1.3cm (½in) above the stumps.

LAW 9 THE BOWLING, POPPING AND RETURN CREASES

The bowling crease shall be marked in line with the stumps at each end and shall be 2.64m (8ft 8in) in length, with the stumps in the centre. The popping crease parallel to it and 1.22m (4ft) nearer the other wicket extends to a minimum of 1.83m (6ft) on either side of centre. (It marks the limit of the ground in which the batsman is safe from being stumped or run out and it is considered to be unlimited in length.)

The return crease shall be at each end of the bowling crease and at right angles to it. (The bowler may not cut the return crease in delivering the ball but must bowl from between the return crease and the stumps.)

LAW 10 ROLLING, SWEEPING, MOWING, WATERING THE PITCH AND RE-MARKING OF CREASES

During the match the pitch may be rolled at the request of the captain of the batting side for not more than seven minutes before the start of each innings. The pitch shall not be watered during a match. Pitch and, when the weather allows, outfield shall be mowed before the start of each day's play. (The other sections of this Law concern the actions which the ground staff may take to maintain the pitch, footholds and crease-markings.)

LAW 11 COVERING THE PITCH

The pitch shall not be completely covered during a match unless prior arrangement or regulations so provide. (In fact, pitches are completely covered almost everywhere now by prior arrangement or regulations, even in England which has often opposed full covering as undermining the character of the game.)

LAW 12 INNINGS

A match shall be of one or two innings of each side according to agreement before the start of play. Each side in a two-innings match takes its innings alternately except where the follow-on is enforced.

LAW 13 THE FOLLOW-ON

In a two-innings match the side which bats first and leads by 200 runs in a five-day match, 150 in a three-day match, 100 in a two-day match or 75 runs in a one-day match may ask the other side to bat again at once. (For this purpose a three-day match becomes a two-day match if the first day is lost through rain.)

THE LAWS OF CRICKET

LAW 14 DECLARATIONS
The captain of the batting side may declare an innings closed at any time.

LAW 15 START OF PLAY
At the start of every session of play the umpire at the bowler's end shall call 'play'. At no time on any day of the match shall there be batting or bowling practice on the pitch. No bowler shall have a trial run-up after 'play' has been called except at the fall of a wicket and then only if the umpire is satisfied that it will cause no waste of time.

LAW 16
The umpire shall allow such intervals as have been agreed upon for meals and ten minutes between each innings. (Intervals are usually a matter for agreement between the two sides and vary throughout the world.)

LAW 17 CESSATION OF PLAY
The umpire at the bowler's end shall call 'time' on the cessation of play, whether before an interval or at the end of the day's play. The umpires then remove the bails from the wickets. (This seemingly trivial formality of calling time achieved great prominence in a Test match in West Indies in 1974 when the batsman, Kallicharran, and some England fielders started to walk off at the close of play but one England fieldsman Greig, threw down the stumps to run out Kallicharran who was by then out of his ground. The umpire's initial ruling that Kallicharran had been run out was later reversed.)

The last over before an interval or the close of play shall be started provided the umpire, after walking at his normal pace, has arrived at his position behind the stumps at the bowler's end before time has been reached. The last over shall be completed unless the batsman is out or retires within two minutes of the scheduled end.

The umpires shall indicate when one hour of playing time remains at the end of a match and 20 six-ball overs or 15 eight-ball overs shall be bowled, if needed, from then. (This has been one of the most successful additions to the Laws throughout the world, putting an end to time-wasting in the last hour and to charges of time-wasting.)

LAW 18 SCORING
A run is scored when the batsmen have crossed and made their ground at the other end or when a boundary is hit or penalty runs are awarded. (Penalty runs include no-balls, wides and the five runs awarded if a fieldsman wilfully stops the ball, other than with any part of his person, eg with his cap, an almost unknown offence.) If the striker is caught, no run is scored. If a batsman is run out, only the run being attempted shall not be scored.

LAW 19 BOUNDARIES
The boundary shall, if possible, be marked by a white line, a rope laid on the ground or a fence. (Law 19 is most often needed when a fieldsman crosses or touches the boundary in stopping or catching the ball. It rules that six runs shall be scored if a fieldsman, after catching the ball, carries it over the boundary. Four runs are scored if a fieldsman with ball in hand grounds any part of his person over the boundary but he is allowed to touch or lean on or over a boundary fence or board in preventing a boundary.)

LAW 20 LOST BALL
If a ball in play cannot be found or recovered, any fieldsman may call 'lost ball' and six runs will be added to the score. If more than six have been run before 'lost ball' is called, as many runs as have been completed shall be scored. (This will presumably only occur in rural areas or where the ball lodges in a tree which is recognised as within the playing area.)

LAW 21 THE RESULT
In two-innings matches the side which has scored a total of runs in excess of that scored by the opposing side in its two completed innings shall be the winners. (That may be a statement of the obvious but Law 21 has also to define a tie. That occurs when the scores are equal but only if the side batting last has completed its innings. Failing that it is a draw. The Law also empowers umpires to award the match to a side whose opponents have refused to play.)

LAW 22 THE OVER
The ball shall be bowled from each wicket alternately in overs of either six or eight balls according to agreement. Neither a wide nor a no-ball shall be reckoned as one of the over. If an umpire miscounts, the over as counted by the umpire shall stand.

LAW 23 DEAD BALL
The ball becomes dead if it is finally settled in the hands of the wicketkeeper or bowler or if it lodges in the clothing of a batsman or umpire. (Most usually this will be in the batsman's pad. It is obviously dead when the umpire calls 'over' and the Law specifies other unusual circumstances in which the umpire should call 'dead ball', as when the bowler drops the ball accidentally before delivery.)

The ball ceases to be dead when the bowler starts his run-up or bowling action. It is not dead when it strikes an umpire, when an unsuccessful appeal is made, when the wicket is broken accidentally by the bowler in delivery or batsman in running or when the wicket is thrown down without the batsman being out.

LAW 24 NO-BALL
The striker shall be out from a no-ball only if he breaks the

THE LAWS OF CRICKET

Laws relating to Hit the Ball Twice, Handling the Ball or Obstructing the Field or if he is run out. (There are various ways in which a no-ball may be bowled, for instance if it is thrown and not bowled with a straight arm. But the cause is nearly always the overstepping by the bowler of the popping crease with the front foot, some part of which, grounded or raised, must be behind the line; or, less frequently, the touching of the return crease with his back foot.)

LAW 25 WIDE-BALL
If the bowler bowls the ball so high over or so wide of the wicket that, in the opinion of the umpire, it passes out of the reach of the striker, standing in a normal guard position, the umpire shall call 'wide-ball'. (The wide, like the no-ball, gives away one run and the ways in which it is possible to be out to a wide are the same.)

LAW 26 BYE AND LEG-BYE
If the striker earns a run without having touched the ball, it is a bye. Leg-byes, off the batsman's dress or person are only scored if the striker has attempted to play the ball or tried to avoid being hit by it.

LAW 27 APPEALS
The umpires shall not give a batsman out unless appealed to by the other side prior to the bowler beginning his run-up or bowling action to deliver the next ball. (An appeal 'How's That?' shall cover all ways of being out. The fielding captain may withdraw an appeal provided the outgoing batsman has not left the field.)

LAW 28 THE WICKET IS DOWN
The wicket is down if either the ball or the striker's bat or person completely removes either bail from the top of the stumps. A disturbance of a bail, whether temporary or not, shall not constitute a complete removal. (This answers the question of whether the wicket is broken if a bail is slightly out of its groove.)

LAW 29 BATSMAN OUT OF HIS GROUND
A batsman is out of his ground unless some part of his bat in hand or of his person is grounded behind the popping crease.

There are ten ways in which a batsman may be out, set out in Laws 30 to 39.

LAW 30 BOWLED
The respective Laws clarify doubtful cases such as when the ball hits the pad before the wicket. The decision is bowled even if the batsman would have been out lbw.

LAW 31 TIMED OUT
An almost unknown offence, which requires the batsman to take more than two minutes to come in and the umpire to be satisfied that the delay is wilful.

LAW 32 CAUGHT
The striker may be caught off the bat or off his hand or glove holding the bat below the wrist (but not off the forearm). A fieldsman must stay within the field of play after making a catch. If he catches the ball off the umpire, it is out but off the helmet of a colleague it is not out.

LAW 33 HANDLED THE BALL
This is a rare offence requiring the batsman to touch the ball wilfully with the hand not holding the bat, perhaps in an instinctive reflex movement intended to protect his wicket.

LAW 34 HIT THE BALL TWICE
Also a very rare way of getting out. A batsman is only allowed to hit the ball twice for the purpose of guarding his wicket. He may be out if he uses his bat to return the ball to a fieldsman but this, though incorrect, is taken as a courtesy and an appeal would be regarded as against the spirit of the game.

LAW 35 HIT WICKET
The striker is out under this Law if the wicket is broken with any part of his person, dress or equipment while making a stroke or setting off for his first run after playing at the ball. He is also out if he hits the wicket when making a second stroke aimed at guarding his wicket.

LAW 36 LEG BEFORE WICKET
A batsman shall be out lbw if a ball which would have hit the wicket hits any part of his person, dress or equipment direct, that is without touching the bat first, provided that:

1. the ball pitched in a straight line between wicket and wicket or on the off side, or in the case of a full pitch would have pitched in a straight line between wicket and wicket; and

2. the point of impact is in a straight line between wicket and wicket even if above the level of the bails. If the batsman has made no genuine attempt to play the ball, he may be out if the point of impact is outside the line of the off stump.

LAW 37 OBSTRUCTING THE FIELD
Another rare offence, this occurs if either batsman wilfully impedes a fieldsman, most likely the wicketkeeper, from making a catch, even though the striker may cause the obstruction in lawfully trying to stop the ball from dropping on to his wicket.

LAW 38 RUN OUT
An unlucky but not infrequent way of being run out is for the bowler to deflect a straight drive involuntarily on to the stumps with the non-striker out of his ground. When both batsmen are out of their ground, the decision as to which is

THE LAWS OF CRICKET

out depends on whether they have crossed when the wicket is put down. If they have crossed, the batsman running towards the broken wicket is out, if not it is his partner. If a batsman remains in his ground or returns to it and his partner joins him there, the latter is out.

LAW 39 STUMPED
The batsman is out stumped if out of his ground when the wicketkeeper breaks the wicket even if the ball has only rebounded from the wicketkeeper's pads. The wicketkeeper may take the ball in front of the wicket in an attempt at a stumping only if it has hit the striker's bat or person.

LAW 40 THE WICKETKEEPER
The wicketkeeper shall remain wholly behind the wicket until the ball has touched the bat or person of the striker or passed the wicket or until the striker attempts a run.

LAW 41 THE FIELDSMAN
The number of on-side fieldsmen behind the popping crease as the ball is bowled shall not exceed two. It if does, the umpire at the striker's end calls 'no-ball'. No fieldsman may have any part of his person over the pitch before the ball has been played or has passed the wicket. (This is designed to prevent both intimidation of the batsman and injury to the fieldsmen.)

LAW 42 UNFAIR PLAY
The captains are responsible at all times for ensuring that play is conducted within the spirit of the game as well as within the Laws. The umpires are the sole judges of fair and unfair play.

(This is easily the most important and far-reaching Law, concerning, as it does, the spirit in which the game is played and involving such difficult and often hard to assess subjects as lifting the seam of the ball, polishing the ball with an artificial substance, obstruction of the batsman in running, excessive bowling of short-pitched balls, time wasting, bowlers following through on to the pitch and the players' general conduct. Where possible, the Laws include notes which provide guidelines to umpires.)

CRICKET TERMS

Backing up This has two senses. The alert non-striker who takes a step or two down the pitch in preparation for a run as the ball is delivered is backing up; and so is the fieldsman who covers another in case he misses the ball.

Back stroke A stroke played with the weight on the back foot usually off a short-pitched ball.

Beamer A fast full pitch which endangers the batsman's head, usually bowled accidentally. It is universally deplored because it is difficult to sight and may cause serious injury.

Block hole The hole made by the batsman just behind the popping crease to mark the guard given him by the umpire.

Bosie In Australia a googly is called a 'bosie' after its inventor in the early 20th century, BJT Bosanquet. See **googly.**

Bouncer The bouncer, or bumper, is a fast short-pitched ball which lifts to the upper part of a batsman's body or above. Much legislation has been directed over the years at restricting short bowling by fast bowlers as being dangerous.

Bump ball A ball hit hard into the ground but which leaps up and may give the appearance of being a catch.

Bumper see **bouncer.**

Call used in three senses. The batsman better placed to see may 'call' his partner for a run. When several fielders converge under a high catch, the captain, to prevent confusion, 'calls' the name of the player to take it. An umpire 'calls' a no-ball, a bowler in this sense is 'called'.

Carry one's bat An opening batsman who is still not out when the last wicket of an innings falls is said to have carried his bat.

Chinaman A ball bowled by a left-arm spin bowler which is an off-break to a right-handed batsman.

Cross bat When the batsman plays across the line of a ball with the bat not perpendicular.

Duck A score of nought. Originating from 'duck's egg', an expression dating back to the 1860s.

Extras Those runs not scored by the batsman, that is byes, leg-byes, wides and no-balls. Called 'sundries' in Australia.

Forward stroke A stroke played with the weight on the front foot, the left foot in the case of a right-handed batsman.

Full pitch or **full toss** A ball which reaches the batsman without touching the ground.

Googly A ball bowled by a right-hand leg-break bowler with what is apparently a leg-break action but which is in fact an off-break. In the case of a left-arm bowler, the googly will be a leg-break bowled with an off-break action. Also called in both cases the 'wrong 'un'.

Green pitch A well-grassed pitch with some moisture in it, likely to favour the faster bowlers, especially early in the day before it has dried out.

Hat-trick The taking of three wickets in successive balls by a bowler. The balls may be split by an intervening over bowled from the other end or indeed by an interval between two innings as long as the innings are in the same match.

Hook A stroke made with weight on the back foot, off a short rising ball which is hit on the leg-side.

Inswinger A ball which swings in the air from the off-side to the leg, that is, into the batsman.

Late cut A stroke played late to a shortish ball outside the off-stump with the weight on the back foot which is thrust over towards the slips. The bat comes down on the ball which should be hit through the slips. A stroke less frequently played in the modern game.

Leg-break A ball which turns from the leg-side to the off and is most frequently associated with a right-arm bowler who turns the wrist over in delivery. However, the term 'leg-break' is also used for the orthodox ball of the left-arm spin bowler.

Leg-cutter Bowled by a bowler of medium-pace and above who cuts his fingers across the seam of the ball and achieves a faster if less sharp version of the leg-break.

Leg-side The side of the playing area behind the batsman as he takes his stance at the crease.

Length A good length ball is one off which the batsman finds it difficult to score because it is neither short enough to cut, hook or play off the back foot nor full enough to drive.

Long hop A short ball allowing the batsman time to cut or hook.

Maiden An over off which no runs are scored. If it also includes the taking of a wicket, it is a 'wicket maiden'.

Night watchman A lower-order batsman sent in prematurely when a wicket falls a few minutes before the close of play to avoid risking one of the better batsmen.

Off-break A ball which turns from off to leg after pitching. Bowled by a right-arm bowler, the ball is gripped between the first and second fingers with the seam usually at right angles between them. The top joint of the first finger is on the seam and the hand turns clockwise as the ball is delivered.

Off-cutter As with the leg-cutter, the bowler cuts his fingers down the side of the ball (the other side) and hopes to produce a fast off-break.

Off-drive A drive off the front foot in front of the wicket on the off-side.

Off-side The side of the field in front of the batsman as he takes his stance at the crease.

On-drive A drive off the front foot in front of the wicket on the on-side, usually between midwicket and the bowler.

Outfield Often referred to as the 'deep'. The playing area nearer the boundary than the pitch.

Outswinger A ball which swings from leg to off in the air, that is, away from the right-handed batsman.

Over the wicket Indicates that the hand with which the bowler, whether right-arm or left-arm, is bowling, is the one nearer the bowler's wicket.

Overthrow A throw at the wicket which is not gathered by other members of the fielding side and goes far enough to allow the batsman to take one more run. It may go to the

CRICKET TERMS

boundary, in which case it is four overthrows, and it counts to the batsman if he hit the ball originally. Overthrows can be run even if the ball has broken the wicket on its course.

Played on When a batsman, officially bowled, has hit the ball on to his wicket.

Pull A shot played by a batsman moving across his wicket to a short ball, perhaps on the line of the off-stump or outside, to the area of midwicket.

Round the wicket Indicates that the hand with which the bowler, whether right-arm or left-arm, is bowling is the one further away from the bowler's wicket.

Seamer Short for seam bowler, a comparatively modern term for a bowler of medium pace or above who aims to make the ball deviate off the pitch by landing it on the seam.

Shine The smooth polished surface of the ball when new is jealously preserved by the faster bowlers especially because it may help the ball to swing.

Shooter A ball which skids along the ground after it pitches and invariably surprises the batsman who has expected it to bounce. The product of a bad pitch, not of the bowler's skill.

Short run If one of the batsmen fails to ground his bat over the popping crease while they are running two or more runs, the umpire signals 'one short'.

Shouldering arms A military term given to the unmilitary manoeuvre by a batsman of raising his bat above his shoulder as he lets a ball pass outside his off-stump without playing a stroke at it.

Square cut Played to a short ball outside the off-stump. The batsman thrusts his back foot across and hits down on the ball, with wrists active, aiming square on the off-side.

Sticky wicket More correctly 'sticky pitch'. The difficult situation in which the batsman found himself in the days of uncovered pitches when, as the sun dried the top of a wet pitch, the ball would turn and lift unpredictably.

Sweep A stroke played at a ball on or outside the leg-stump with the front leg thrust forward and the bat coming down round it until after impact the bat is parallel to the ground.

Tail Late-order batsmen and generally not very good ones.

Top spin Spin imparted by slow bowlers which makes the ball bounce more and perhaps faster than expected without deviating off line.

Track Slang expression for a pitch.

Twelfth man Substitute fieldsman.

Wrong 'un see **googly.**

Yorker A ball pitched near the batsmen's feet which, if he misjudges it or is surprised by the pace of it, may pass under his bat. A straight yorker fired by a very fast bowler can be a deadly weapon and a bowler below top pace may often profit from the element of surprise in a yorker.